Music in Philadelphia

Annals of Music in Philadelphia and History of the Musical Fund Society

From its Organization in 1820 to the year 1858

Compiled by

Louis C. Madeira

Edited by

Philip H. Goepp

Ross & Perry, Inc.
Washington, D.C.

Copyright, 1896, J. B. Lippincott Company
Reprinted by Ross & Perry, Inc. 2002
© Ross & Perry, Inc. 2002 on new material. All rights reserved.

Protected under the Berne Convention.

Printed in The United States of America

Ross & Perry, Inc. Publishers
216 G St., N.E.
Washington, D.C. 20002
Telephone (202) 675-8300
Facsimile (202) 675-8400
info@RossPerry.com

SAN 253-8555

Library of Congress Control Number: 2002116989
http://www.rossperry.com

ISBN 1-932109-44-7

Book Cover designed by Sapna. sapna@rossperry.com

✆ The paper used in this publication meets the requirements for permanence established by the American National Standard for Information Sciences "Permanence of Paper for Printed Library Materials" (ANSI Z39.48-1984).

All rights reserved. No copyrighted part of this publication may be reproduced, stored in a retrieval system, or transmitted, in any form or by any means, electronic, photocopying, recording, or otherwise, without the prior written permission of the publisher.

CONTENTS

CHAPTER I.   Page
    Early Conditions: Church Music: Bishop White 17

CHAPTER II.
    Earliest Dramatic Entertainments: Prejudice against the Theatre: Legislation: Local Musicians 26

CHAPTER III.
    Instruments: First Piano-forte: Benjamin Franklin: Musical Glasses: Eminent Musicians: Societies 46

CHAPTER IV.
    Beginnings of the Musical Fund Society . 57

CHAPTER V.
    Early Years of the Musical Fund Society . 78

CHAPTER VI.
    Building of the Hall 93

CHAPTER VII.
    Early Plans and Experiments of the Society 102

CONTENTS

CHAPTER VIII. Page
    Figures of the Time 113

CHAPTER IX.
    English Musicians in Philadelphia . . 123

CHAPTER X.
    Summus Parnassus 142

CHAPTER XI.
    Enlargement of the Hall: The Bazaar: Two Great Pianists 157

CHAPTER XII.
    The Age of Song: Sontag and Lind: The Future 164

ADDENDUM.
    List of Members of the Musical Fund Society and of Officers, with the Date of Tenure, elected between 1820 and 1858 . 176

INDEX 197

ILLUSTRATIONS

BENJAMIN CARR.   Page
    From mezzotint by John Sartain, of painting
    by J. C. Darley   .   .   .   Frontispiece.

RIGHT REV. WILLIAM WHITE, D.D.
    From engraving by R. W. Dodson, of painting by H. Inman 20

MUSICAL FUND HALL
    Before the last alterations 59

PROGRAMME OF SECOND PERFORMANCE OF FIRST CONCERT.
    Reduced fac-simile of first page . . . 70

PROGRAMME OF EIGHTH CONCERT.
    Reduced fac-simile of first page . . . 103

MME. MALIBRAN.
    From a contemporary lithograph . . . 108

S. THALBERG.
    From a contemporary lithograph . . . 125

GIULIA GRISI.
    From the portrait by Negelen, engraved by F. C. Lewis 139

MEIGNIN'S SINFONIA.
    Humorous Sketch of Stage and Orchestra. 144

ILLUSTRATIONS

	Page
PROGRAMME OF OLE BULL'S SECOND CONCERT. Reduced fac-simile.	149
VIEUXTEMPS'S CONCERT. Fac-simile of ticket	154
THE BAZAAR ALBUM. Reduced fac-simile of first page	158
JENNY LIND. From mezzotint by John Sartain, after a daguerreotype by Richards	160
PROGRAMME OF MME. SONTAG'S EXTRA CONCERT. Reduced fac-simile	165
MME. SONTAG AS DONNA ANNA. From the mezzotint by F. Girard, after the painting by Paul Delaroche	169
PROGRAMME OF ADELINA PATTI'S SECOND CONCERT. Reduced fac-simile of first portion	174

EDITOR'S PREFACE

WE are apt, in America, to look forward too exclusively,—to think we have no history. We forget that we have had a culture in the past, of which we may be proud for its own sake, from which we may gather encouragement and inspiration.

Musical culture to-day is an easier matter than it was a century ago. In the sensational, almost too emotional character of modern music there is an appeal as much to the senses as to the mind. There is an orgy of passive enjoyment, rather than the clear thought of poetry.

It does not require, nor does it make for culture in the hearer. In short, the musical enthusiasm to-day in our great cities is a less perfect measure of that particular state of mental and moral development. The musical life in early Philadelphia was of the same cast as was the high atmosphere of the Utopians at Concord. The sphere and the scope of the Philadelphia musicians

EDITOR'S PREFACE

were, of course, much more limited. But we have a right to the same sort of pride in their work as Massachusetts has in its Transcendentalists. The works introduced by Hupfeld and Carr were the same to which to-day we turn with deepest reverence. But in those days they were not hallowed by the consecration of a century's increasing appreciation. Then it needed genuine courage of conviction, genuine musical perception, to play them.

Around music clusters much of the actual feeling of the past,—the view of life, whether serious or gay, of amusement, of art. Its history gauges the mental scope of former generations; it shows the extent to which religion and church-life absorbed thought; how these gradually and increasingly permitted the romantic stimulus to secular thought and feeling abroad to rouse the citizens from the quiet routine of their provincialism. Thus there are several stages of distinct individuality in such a history as ours:

First. When music was viewed as a Bohemian, semi-respectable dissipation. This attitude was due in part to the strict tone of Quaker tradition, in part to the quality of the music that actually reached the city.

EDITOR'S PREFACE

Second. When, under the stimulus of revolution at home and abroad, under the influence of a growing intellectual freedom and scope, prejudices melted away, music and the other arts were actually encouraged.

Third. The transmission of the impetus of the great classic masters.

Fourth. The age of the great virtuosi, —instrumental and vocal. The establishment of permanent institutions for the production of musical master-works.

It is of common acceptance that the homogeneous quality which made us distinctively one nation has now largely disappeared, owing to constant introduction of foreign multitudes which we cannot assimilate. Inland cities have been thought less affected by this evil than seaports. In reality it is doubtful whether there is any difference. Philadelphia has now a hopelessly conglomerate population. Hence there is a peculiar interest in the culture of old times. It represents a memorable period of national development, and of its expression in the arts. Of this culture Philadelphia was the centre. A look into the past, while it will rouse the pride of Philadelphians, must fill them with a certain wistful wonderment as to their future destiny. If it is merely the general blight

EDITOR'S PREFACE

of immigration, which has robbed them of artistic hegemony, there is no reason to doubt a recovery after the period of assimilation. Nor does it seem that the passing of commercial supremacy eastward will permanently affect the question of literary and artistic leadership. A city cannot be given over to both trade and art, each in the highest degree, any more than can an individual.

Thus a glance at earlier times gives courage and confidence for the future. Even now the signs of a new civic vigor are growing in literature, in painting, and in music. The very leisure with which Philadelphia is taunted, is the best condition for the concentration necessary for creative work. In so far our present conditions are like those of the whole country when our literary classics were written. Unfortunately the reception and appreciation of our work is found elsewhere. Hence Philadelphia cannot as yet claim the credit of her own artistic product. There must first come a greater pervading culture throughout the population. The intellectual life of a city depends principally not upon her workers, but upon the general tone which appreciates, stimulates, and rewards the former. In these days we are wont to

EDITOR'S PREFACE

solve every problem with the cheque of rich individuals. We are in danger of a greater as a more vulgar system of patronage than in the worst days of Chesterfield and of Grubb Street.

In olden times there was a democracy of culture. There was no unwashed horde. A record of musical doings is true of the whole community, not of a small circle. It is this which must be our aim, now and always: not the support of an institution by the wealthy few, but the gradual education of all, as the only permanent soil for a higher æsthetic life. To look elsewhere for a lasting foundation would be much the same folly as that of a church seeking the support of a few rich men, indifferent to the number of its members.

PHILIP H. GOEPP.

Since the beginning of this work, the compiler, Louis C. Madeira, has passed away. The collection of facts, illustrations, and other materials for a musical history was for years his favorite occupation. Its final publication was, perhaps, his most absorbing wish.

It was, probably, his connection with the Musical Fund Society that first suggested

EDITOR'S PREFACE

the idea, as it gave opportunity for its fulfilment. His membership began in the season of 1843-44. Soon he became one of the managers. At the great Bazaar in 1847, in the acme of the Society's career, he was one of the moving spirits. He represented the Society during the memorable reception given to Madame Sontag in 1852, personally bringing the singer's party to the city. He was Secretary of the Society from 1856-1858.

ANNALS OF MUSIC IN PHILADELPHIA

CHAPTER I. EARLY CONDITIONS: CHURCH MUSIC: BISHOP WHITE

THROUGHOUT the first century of the history of Philadelphia the conditions for the development of musical and literary taste were most inauspicious. Public feeling or demand for such expression may be said to have been at a point below zero. In religion and in politics, opposition and interdiction often supply an unwilling stimulus. It is not so in art.

The only evidence of musical entertainments in Philadelphia before the middle of the eighteenth century is of a negative kind. In 1716, at the Yearly Meeting of the Friends, members were advised against "going to or being in any way concerned in plays, games, lotteries, music, and dancing." It seems probable that this was intended, if not as rebuke for actual indulgence, at least as a practical prohibition

MUSIC IN PHILADELPHIA

rather than mere enunciation of an abstract principle.

The development of a musical desire in Philadelphia was one long struggle against Quaker tradition and regulation. It is significant that it was in the church that music found her first refuge there, as it was in the church that she was originally reared. Slowly it dawned upon those early purists that divine worship lost none of its seriousness by invoking the aid of music for its expression. Then came the final discovery that even secular music might not be hostile to a wholesome civic life,—nay, that in its masterpieces might lie the expression of just such a sentiment as that which drove the Quakers to their colonial settlement.

Christ Church, founded in 1695, was the first Episcopal Church in Philadelphia. Its service was, of course, that of the Church of England. In September, 1728, within a year after the present building was begun, a new organ was purchased for £200, Peter Brayton and others being a committee to procure subscriptions for its purchase and erection. It is inferred that there must have been an organ of some kind before. In November, 1763, a subscription was obtained for the purchase of an organ from Philip Feying, who had built one for St.

EARLY MUSIC

Peter's. The vestry of Christ Church, in April, 1764, were impressed with the efforts of William Young and Francis Hopkinson in teaching the children of the united congregations of their own church and of St. Peter's the art of psalmody, and expressed their acknowledgments. In 1770, Francis Hopkinson, having played the organ during the absence of Mr. Bremmer, the organist, was requested to continue in the office as long as it was convenient to him. John Bankson was at that time organist at St. Peter's. On the 4th of June, 1782, the vestry ordered that an orchestra be erected in front of the gallery where the organ stands, for the convenience of a number of singers; and in April, 1785, the clerks were requested to sing such tunes only as "are plain and familiar to the congregation; the frequent changing of tunes being generally disagreeable."

Bishop White appears early in the new century as the strong champion of music in the Episcopal service, parrying the existing prejudice by his high conception of its function and by the severity with which he denounced its abuse.

In a report made to the general convention in 1808 is the following: " . . . as it is by the Gospel that life and immortality are brought to light: there would seem to be a suitableness to its high design in celebrating its prominent subjects in definite terms, so that many edifying events, embodied with Christian doctrine and essential to it, may reasonably be rendered the more impressive by their being carried to the heart on the wings of poetry and music."

In a pamphlet on "Thoughts on the Singing of the Psalms and Anthems in Churches," Bishop White, in 1808, marks the "distinction . . . between the making of devotion pleasing by the aid of music and the applying of music to convey a pleasure not intended to be instrumental to devotion." Further on he says, "concerning interludes and voluntaries" that "nothing contrary either to good taste or decency should be tolerated for the gratification of private whim, much less in violation of all regard to religion and decorum." He inveighs against the "licentiousness . . . conspicuous in some places, in those light airs, which are calculated to send people dancing out of the church." He adds that "it is well known that some members of congregations have been occasionally offended by seeing persons exhibited in their orchestras as singers who never appear in any church at any other time, and whose

EARLY MUSIC

occupation, to say the least, is unfavorable to piety and morals." In a letter to Dr. Abercrombie, 1807, Bishop White speaks of himself as "having been, so far as I know, the first clergyman in the United States who introduced chaunting into any of our churches." He adds, in apologetic spirit, "We sing in translation. Now if it be found, on experience, as is the fact, that rhyme, especially in the English language, makes the composition agreeable to the ear, it is difficult to see what principle is endangered by condescending to the well-known taste of Christians generally in this respect." The first Roman Catholic church in the United States was St. Joseph's, Willing's Alley. The first church building was erected in 1730. The church records having been lost or destroyed, little information can be obtained relating to the musical part of the services. Mention is made of an organ having been in the church in 1748–50, and the one used in 1780 is still in existence. The Rev. Robert Harding took charge of the church in 1750, and the music of the services was under the care of a cultivated musician. The choir was composed of the best voices obtainable, and new voices were sought for whenever there was an opportunity.

MUSIC IN PHILADELPHIA

It has been stated that Lafayette, the Counts de Rochambeau and de la Grasse, and other French officers of the Revolution attended services at St. Joseph's.

The church was illuminated on March 1, 1781, and a Te Deum was chanted, celebrating the ratification of the "alliance and perpetual union of the States." Monsieur de la Luzerne, the French minister, with his suite, was present.

At one time Benjamin Carr was the organist.

During the sitting of the Constitutional Convention, Washington, in his diary, mentions having attended a high mass at St. Joseph's Church on Sunday, May 27, 1787.

"In the Presbyterian Church," it is recorded, "the precentor, or singing leader, was an important officer. His manner of leading the tunes was as integral a part of the service as the text and method of the sermon. He stood beneath the pulpit, with a tuning-fork in his hand, at a table or desk placed on a slight elevation from the church floor, and lined out the hymns."* The singing, in which the congregation joined, consisted generally of a simple melody in unison. Here and there might

---

* Scharf and Westcott's History of Philadelphia.

EARLY MUSIC

be heard parts of the harmony, sung by those who had confidence enough to make themselves conspicuous. When the leader had sung his first note and was about to begin his second, down at the farther end of the church they were starting on the first note, much like the falling of bricks set on end. Congregational singing was a duty with Presbyterians. In his home the church-member abstained from the use of musical instruments.

The need of some harmonic instrumental support evidently suggested the use of the bass-viol. Its introduction into the church met with vigorous opposition, especially on the part of the ministers. To one of these Tories a singer, wishing to improve on the lines on Dr. Watt's ninety-second psalm—

>"Oh, let my heart in tune be found
>Like David's harp, of solemn sound"—

gravely proposed this change:

>"Oh, may my heart be tuned within
>Like David's sacred violin!"

to which the reverend wag suggested as amendment:

>"Oh, may my heart go diddle-diddle
>Like Uncle David's sacred fiddle."

MUSIC IN PHILADELPHIA

The Baptists sang hymns in their services, as did the German Reformed body, while the music of the Swedes and of the Lutherans resembled that of the Anglican church.

The Moravians were noted for the excellence of the musical part of their religious services. In the eighteenth century, when Philadelphia easily surpassed New York in musical culture, the highest musical activity in the country existed in Bethlehem, the episcopal seat of the Moravians. They used in their services (as they still do today), besides the organ, brass and stringed instruments, such as trumpets, trombones, clarionets, the harp, violins, and bass-viols. This shocked the Friends and Presbyterians, to whom the organ was "a box of whistles." In the Moravian Church, at the corner of Race and Broad Streets, there were two organs in 1743. The principal one, growing old, was sold in 1796, and its place soon supplied by a new instrument, made by David Tannenberg. In 1808 still another organ, built by John Schermer, was purchased for $280. The Second Moravian Church was furnished in 1805 with an organ made by E. W. Scherr.

John Adams, in his diary in 1774, says he found the chanting in the Catholic

EARLY MUSIC

Church in Philadelphia "exquisitely soft and sweet." The fervent emotional singing of the newly-settled Methodists also impressed him deeply. He describes it as "the finest music I have heard in any society except the Moravians, and once in a church with an organ."

Typical of the violent opposition to the organ in church is the remark of a preacher, who, asked to lead in prayer after the organ had been heard with the singers, cried out, " Call on the machine! If it can sing and play to the glory of God, it can pray to the glory of God also. Call on the machine!"

MUSIC IN PHILADELPHIA

CHAPTER II. EARLIEST DRAMATIC ENTERTAINMENTS: PREJUDICE AGAINST THE THEATRE: LEGISLATION: LOCAL MUSICIANS

THE first stirrings of a desire for public entertainment other than cock-fights, rope-dances, and the exhibition of monstrosities, to which the pious attitude of the Friends had restricted the community, appear about the middle of the eighteenth century. There are traces of an association "formed in the city for musical purposes, and also a dancing assembly," composed, it is said, of prominent men, nearly all being members of the Church of England. "Music masters" announce themselves, who teach "the violin, hautboy, common flute, and dulcimer, by note." Sometimes they eke out their nascent trade by the more respectable vocation of drawing bonds and leases.

Undoubtedly the earliest dramatic performances took place in "William Plumstead's warehouse, in King (now Water) Street, below Pine." The time and the

EARLY MUSIC

names of plays and players are less certain. There seems to have been a short-lived attempt in 1749, by the English actors Murray and Kean, who were probably assisted by some local amateurs, to take a stand against traditions and authorities. The common opinion, however, which ascribes to the Hallam Company of English actors the first ambitious dramatic enterprise in America is, in the main, right, but it is difficult to tell which particular Hallam deserves the magnificent title of "Father of the American stage;" whether William, the manager, who, staying at home, conceived and organized the undertaking; Lewis, his brother, the actor, who launched it successfully; or Lewis, Jr., the latter's son, who, for full half a century, was the leading actor in America. The original company was not without repute in London. Perhaps they felt the shadow of the coming Garrick. Their plays, well-learned before embarking, included "The Merchant of Venice," "Richard the Third," "Hamlet," and "Othello," together with a number of pieces of the day. In all, the plays with the farces, which invariably followed the former, numbered twenty-four. Of these farces, some, like Cibber's "Hob in the Well," are spoken of as operas,—which

MUSIC IN PHILADELPHIA

can mean nothing more than a sprinkling of ballads throughout the play.

After a successful season in Williamsburg, Virginia, where the company opened with "The Merchant of Venice," on September 5, 1752, and another in New York, Lewis Hallam procured, with the assistance of many petitioners from Philadelphia, opposed by an almost equal number, permission from Governor Hamilton, of Pennsylvania, to act twenty-four plays and farces, not without strict provision against anything "indecent or immoral." The permission seems to have been sought from a general foreboding of difficulties rather than from knowledge of actual legal restriction. Perhaps it was granted because it could not lawfully have been withheld. The season began on April 25, 1754, in the warehouse on Water Street, described above, with the play, "The Fair Penitent," followed by "Miss in her Teens." The play nights were Mondays, Wednesdays, and Fridays. The ladies sent their negro servants to keep their places from four o'clock until six, when the curtain rose, or until their mistresses came. The strife raged fiercely. The champions, it seems, were chiefly of the members of the Church of England; the opponents were mainly

EARLY MUSIC

Presbyterians and Quakers. In two papers —Franklin's "Pennsylvania Gazette," and Bradford's "Pennsylvania Journal"— one "A. B." attacked the stage generally. He was answered the following week by "Y. Z." in Franklin's "Gazette." Play-bills, advertisements, prologues, and epilogues (which were never omitted), all betray the state of feeling in their apologetic tone. On May 27, 1754, at the "New Theatre in Water Street," the after-piece was a "ballad opera," called "The Country Wake," or, "Hob in the Well," which was, of course, no more than a farce, with songs interspersed.

The company disappeared for a number of years. On returning to Philadelphia, Douglass, who had succeeded Lewis Hallam as manager at the latter's death, erected a frame building at the southwest corner of South and Vernon Streets, in a region called Society Hill. The theatre was just outside of the city limits in Southwark. We are told that it cost "upwards of £300." The contest against the imported corruption was steadily maintained. Laws against plays were regularly passed in the colonies, and rejected by the council in England. It was not without true courage that Judge Allen, petitioned for an injunction to restrain the players, refused, saying that he had received "more moral virtue from plays than sermons."

A second theatre was built in Southwark in 1766, on South Street, between Fourth and Fifth, at the corner of a small street since called Apollo. This was long known as the "Old South Street Theatre." The company, of which the young Lewis Hallam was now the leading member, is from this time called "The American Company."

Much importance is given by some chroniclers to the performance, by Hallam's Company at the New Theatre on Society Hill in 1759, of "Theodosius," as the first attempt at opera, followed soon after by Gay's "Beggar Opera." These representations, without the slightest claim to serious musical standard, show the gradual growth of a musical desire. Of similar significance is a performance of Arne's "Masque of Alfred," in 1757, by the students of the College of Philadelphia. "Several young ladies," it is reported, "condescended to sing the songs."

Another occasion when amateurs appeared in public was "an interlude of concert music," in December, 1759, performed by "some gentlemen of the city," for the purpose of "purchasing an organ for the

EARLY MUSIC

College Hall in this city, and instructing the college children in psalmody." A "concert of musical glasses," in 1765, was a success. The singers were of Douglass' Company, of which the members, we are told, "contributed not a little to increase the taste for music."

An announcement in the "Pennsylvania Journal," in the fall of 1764, reads: "Subscription Concert at the Assembly Room, Lodge Alley, begins on Thursday, the 8th of November next, to continue every other Thursday till the 14th of March following. Each subscriber on paying three pounds to be entitled to two Ladies' tickets for the season. The concert to begin precisely at six o'clock in the evening. Tickets to be had at the bar of the London Coffee House."

Another concert, given in 1764, was thus advertised:

"For the benefit of Mr. Forage and others, assistant performers at the Subscription Concerts in this city, on Monday, 31st instant, at the Assembly Room, on Lodge Alley, will be performed

A Concert of Music,

consisting of a variety of the most celebrated pieces now in taste, in which will be introduced the famous Armonica or Musical glasses, so much admired for the

MUSIC IN PHILADELPHIA

great Sweetness and Delicacy of its tone. Tickets at 7/6 each, to be had at the bar of the London Coffee House. No person to be admitted without a Ticket. The concert to begin at six o'clock precisely."

So in 1770, Signor Gualdo announces "a concert of vocal and instrumental music, solos and concertos in various instruments, the favorite mandolin not excepted."

During most of the time the American Company, which seemed to be the sole source of dramatic entertainment, was playing at the Southwark Theatre, with intervals of absences in New York and in smaller cities. The fanatical spirit still prevailed. But it does not seem to have extended to music. On the contrary, restrictions against plays were commonly avoided under the disguise of "concerts."

On March 22, 1770, Milton's masque "Comus" was given by the Hallam Company. 1773 was probably their last season of plays. The Continental Congress in 1774 passed a resolution "discouraging every species of extravagance and dissipation, especially horse-racing, and all kinds of gaming, cock-fighting, exhibitions of shows, plays, and other expensive diversions and entertainments." The course of political events tended greatly to help the side of the

EARLY MUSIC

purists. A growing political independence gave greater weight to the resolutions of public bodies; the sense of the coming stress, of the necessity of concentrated effort, left little spirit or resources for public amusements. The only break in the long absence of gayety was a season of amateur drama by the British officers under General Howe, who occupied Philadelphia during the winters of 1777-78. Their forcible possession of city and play-house did not prevent an appreciative reception on the part of many of the citizens. A somewhat ironical stroke of fate, connected with this chapter of Philadelphia history, is the story that a drop-scene, painted by the unfortunate Major André for the military actors, was actually used some twenty years later as the scene of his own capture in a play written on the subject.

On the 12th of October, 1778, Congress found it necessary to recommend that the several States pass laws to prevent theatrical entertainments, "and such other diversions as are productive of idleness." Direct penalty of dismissal was enacted against United States officials who encouraged plays. The preamble shows that the reason was a temporary one, the need of concentration on the common defence.

MUSIC IN PHILADELPHIA

While there was no actual prohibition, yet players were almost as much in awe of public opinion as of the law itself. This state lasted for years after the war had ended. Not until 1790 was there a regular, frankly announced season of drama, again by the American Company at the Southwark Theatre. But throughout the period there are quaint evasions of the law (real or supposed), yet with shamefaced apologies.

On March 12, 1785, Hallam opened the Southwark with "Lectures, moral and entertaining." Durang tells us that they "consisted of scenes out of plays, scraps of pantomimes, dancing, and singing."* The "Pennsylvania Mercury" approved. There was a series of curious miscellaneous "attractions." A puppet "opera," "The Poor Soldier," with the singers behind the scenes, was a great success in 1787. Better than description is the bill for June 23, 1787, which reads:

SPECTACULUM VITÆ

At the Opera House,
Southwark,
For the Relief of our Fellow Citizens
Enslaved at
ALGIERS.

---

* Durang's History of the Philadelphia Stage.

EARLY MUSIC

On Monday next
Will be performed
A CONCERT,
Vocal and Instrumental,
In the first part of which will be introduced
THE GRATEFUL WARD;
Or, The Pupil in Love.
And in the second part will be presented the Musical Entertainment of the
POOR SOLDIER,
with the original overture, accompaniment, songs, and new scenery.

A poetical address, composed for the occasion, will be delivered at the opening of the entertainment, and the whole will conclude with an elegant
VAUD-VILLE.

N.B.—The managers of this entertainment, solicitious of contributing towards the relief of the unfortunate American captives in Algiers, have cheerfully complied with the request of many respectable citizens upon this occasion, and having diligently endeavored to render the Opera House as cool as commodious, they purpose stopping a fortnight in this city, on their way to Baltimore. During this short stay they hope to merit and receive the patronage and appreciation of the public.

The doors will be opened at half-past six o'clock, and the concert to begin precisely at half-past seven.

. . . Ladies and gentlemen are requested to send their servants in time to keep their boxes. Box, 7s. 6d.; Pit, 5s.; Gallery, 3s. 9d.

So a play—"The Gamester"—is thus an-

MUSIC IN PHILADELPHIA

nounced: "Between the parts of the concert will be presented a serious and moral lecture in five parts, on the sin of gambling, at the request of several ladies and gentlemen." Hamlet was a "moral and instructive tale, . . . introduced between the parts of the concert, . . . called Filial Piety Exemplified in the History of the Prince of Denmark."

A genuine "Grand Concert of Sacred Song" was given on May 4, 1786, at the Reformed German Church, on Race Street, for the benefit of the Pennsylvania Hospital, Philadelphia Dispensary, and the Poor."

Among the numbers in the "order of music" are: "Martini's celebrated overture," a flute and a violin concerto, both by obscure Miltons, five anthems, and, at the close, Händel's Hallelujah Chorus from the "Messiah." One of the anthem composers, W. Billings, of Boston, seems to have been of much importance. He is often called "the first American composer."

The prohibition of theatres, together with the energetic management of a Mr. Adgate, with a chorus of two hundred and thirty voices, and a band of fifty instruments, united to make it successful and eventful.

In Washington's diary he mentions attending, during the Constitutional Conven-

EARLY MUSIC

tion, a benefit concert for Mr. Juhan, at the City Tavern, on May 29, 1787. Again there is the grand overture of Martini, and a sonata by Haydn, quite significant of improved taste. It must have been a sonata for violin and piano, played on the harpsichord. Besides the real music, there is always a plentiful display of "overtures" and "concertos" by the local geniuses. Among the Juhans, Reinagles, and Browns, there is scant room for a Haydn. This was partly due to the old tradition that a musician must be a composer, partly to the difficulty of procuring the great musical works. We must content ourselves with wondering whether the audience perceived the difference between Haydn and Reinagle. In justice much is owed to the pioneers who were guiding the public in the right way, in the days when there were no acknowledged "Masters."

Again, we have evidence that the illustrious Father of his Country bowed to the humanizing influence of the stage. This was at the Southwark Theatre, where Washington attended three performances. In his diary it is recorded that, to mitigate the exactions of the Constitutional Convention, on the 10th of July he witnesses "High Life below Stairs," and the second act of the "Poor Soldier." This must have been the first time Washington ever saw O'Keefe's comedy; but it continued to be a favorite with him. On the 14th instant he again attended the play. This time it was a production of Dryden's version of the "Tempest," and the interlude of "Neptune and Amphitrite." Finally, on the 21st of the same month, he enjoys Thomson's prohibited tragedy, "Edward and Eleonora."

From this time on there is besides "operas and musical pieces" at the Southwark, a new series of musical entertainment at Harrowgate Garden, near Frankford.

In 1796 concerts and exhibitions were given in Andrew Hamilton's Mansion, Bush Hill, under the direction of John Darley, from Birmingham, England, who owned the mansion; but the enterprise was not successful. Bush Hill was built by Andrew Hamilton, who died in 1741, a year after it was completed. It stood on the north side of what is now Buttonwood Street, between Seventeenth and Eighteenth Streets. It was burned in 1808. From it Hamilton Street derives its name.

There was also a Northern Liberties Theatre opened in 1791.

EARLY MUSIC

A new epoch begins with the erection of the Chestnut Street Theatre, near Sixth. It must have been of architectural merit. It is described as presenting "a handsome front on Chestnut Street of ninety feet, including two wings of fifteen feet. The centre building is ornamented with two spirited and well-executed figures of Tragedy and Comedy, on each side of the great Venetian window, over which, in two circular tablets, are emblematical insignia." It was said to have been modelled from the Bath Theatre in England. To test the qualities of the new house, the managers gave, in April, 1793, a "grand concert of vocal and instrumental music." The first dramatic performance (delayed by the yellow-fever epidemic) in February, 1794, was of the English "opera" "The Castle of Andalusia," followed by a farce. All the appointments of the house and of the company were of the highest standard then known. Reinagle was evidently the chief musical figure of the day. The leader of the orchestra was George Gillingham, "the celebrated violinist from London," under whom, we are told, there were "about twenty accomplished musicians," who were "deemed equal in general ability with the stage artists." The criticism of a contemporary has an unconscious value, especially when it is considered that the operas were merely connected plays with familiar songs set here and there. Our critic gently disapproves the tendency of the managers to push the operatic entertainments at the expense of tragedy and comedy. "The country," he adds, "at that period had not made any advances in the more scientific music of the lyrical style, however au fait in judgment our audience was in the regular drama. Music of an elevated character, to be properly appreciated, must have adequate judges, which only old and refined nations can furnish in sufficient numbers to support so expensive an institution as opera." *

So, on the performance of "Robin Hood" in 1794, he says, "The day had not arrived for operatic speculations. Music is only now (1850) progressing with us to a just appreciation, induced by the more elevated compositions of the Italian school." He speaks doubtfully of the distant prospect of "a just musical taste." His only hope is in Italian influence.

It is clear that the taste of the day reflected faintly that of London. The only

---

* Durang's "History of the Philadelphia Stage."

EARLY MUSIC

music that really appealed to public taste was that of English ballads, introduced in English operas. There was, besides, an incipient appreciation of some of the German masters, like Händel and Haydn, who had visited England, and had succeeded, by careful wooing, in conquering English recognition. The way to which the worthy critic points as the ideal was, in reality, a backward step. It was the overwhelming triumph of the superficial Italian school, checking the study of the great German classics, which must account for a certain chronic lack of seriousness in our musical life. That early period, when the German masters were introduced and studied before their greatness was blazoned abroad, is one to which we can look with most pride, wishing it might have continued and averted a later degeneration.

Probably as the first performance of oratorio, Händel's "Messiah" was given in 1801 in the hall of the University of Pennsylvania. The soloists were recruited from the Chestnut Street Theatre. Among them were Mrs. Oldmixon, one of the leading members, who was the first to sing the "Blue Bells of Scotland" in Philadelphia. Her husband, Sir John Oldmixon, performed on the violin. Later, Mrs. Old-

MUSIC IN PHILADELPHIA

mixon kept a ladies' seminary at Germantown. A similar concert in 1810 seems to have been long considered a famous occasion. While no entire choral work was sung, the programme consisting of certain numbers from Händel's "Messiah" and from Haydn's "Creation," the magnitude of the preparations, the size of the orchestra, the number of prominent musicians who took part, mark it as the result of the united musical aspirations and efforts of the time. We are told that "thirty-four ladies and gentlemen sang in the principal parts and chorus. The orchestra was exceedingly strong, much beyond the usual number of the orchestras of that time." Besides twenty-one violins and a corresponding proportion of larger strings, there was the extraordinary number of four clarionets and six flutes.

Among the names of the leaders are some that are still spoken of with enthusiasm. Above all, the personality of Benjamin Carr stands out as one who, of all the early musicians of Philadelphia, wrought most vigorously to introduce the best, chiefly in the oratorio and in the church. An Englishman of breeding and education, he was of a type in which Philadelphia has been fortunately rich. Carr and

EARLY MUSIC

Schetky had a music-store on Fifth Street before 1800.

Raynor Taylor was an organist who seems to have been very prominent. Vauxhall Garden, on the northeast corner of Broad and Walnut Streets, was opened for concerts and other entertainments in May, 1814. On one of the programmes it is promised "that the temple and garden will be brilliantly illuminated with variegated lamps. Admission, $1. . . . Smoking is not permitted in or near the temple." Taylor was organist on the opening night. Gillingham was the regular conductor. On one programme Taylor appears twice as composer and Gillingham once. The only familiar names are Pleyel and Kreutzer. Most of the numbers are patriotic songs, overtures, and grand marches; the finale is "The Columbian's March to Glory," written by a gentleman of Philadelphia. The garden was the great resort; one of the round of entertainments at Lafayette's second visit in 1825 was held there.

Besides the members of the Chestnut Street Theatre Company, who were constantly in demand for public singing, there were prominent concert musicians at that time, such as Charles P. Hupfeld, a violinist, and Francis Blondan, a flutist.

MUSIC IN PHILADELPHIA

A musical organization of small pretensions but of very considerable celebrity was Johnson's Band, which came into notice about 1815. It was organized and led by Francis Johnson, a colored man. In his early career he played the trumpet; but later he performed on the Kent bugle, which at that time became very popular. At this instrument he was considered the equal of Willis, the leader of the band at the West Point Military Academy. Willis's reputation was very high.

In spite of race prejudice, Johnson managed, by musical talent and natural ability, together with a strong personal tact, to make himself a notability in his line. Without aspirations for classic music, he had an excellent ear for melody and a facility for preparing military music and for changing popular airs. He could turn the most melancholy refrain into a cotillon. He also wrote many original marches and dances, and had some ingenuity in inventing quadrille music with novel features. One of them was the "voice quadrilles," in which the band suddenly burst forth singing in chorus. He called around him a number of men of his own color, who were self-taught but competent players. Johnson's sphere lay chiefly in military music and in

EARLY MUSIC

the ball-room; for many years his band was the only one employed on parade by the State Fencibles, and was in great demand for fashionable dances. In 1825 and during many subsequent years it was a recognized attraction at Saratoga. It furnished the music at the Lafayette reception ball in 1824 at the Chestnut Street Theatre, for which occasion Johnson wrote special numbers. In 1837, Johnson visited Europe with his band, and performed, it is said, to royal audiences. But during a visit of the Fencibles to Boston the band was not allowed to play in Providence, Rhode Island, on account of their color.

MUSIC IN PHILADELPHIA

CHAPTER III. INSTRUMENTS: FIRST PIANO-FORTE: BENJAMIN FRANKLIN: MUSICAL GLASSES: EMINENT MUSICIANS: SOCIETIES.

IN a recently published life of Lafayette there is the recorded impression of a French nobleman, the Marquis de Chastellux, of a musical afternoon. It gives a glimpse of the principal musical instruments of a Philadelphia household in 1780. The Marquis and Lafayette went to take tea at Mrs. Shippen's. "This is the first time since my arrival in America that I have seen music appear in society, and mingle with amusements. Miss Rutledge played on the harpsichord, and played very well. Miss Shippen sang timidly, but had an attractive voice. Mr. Ottaw, secretary to the Chevalier de la Luzerne, had his harp brought, accompanied Miss Shippen, and also played some pieces. Music naturally leads to dancing; the Vicomte de Noailles strung some harp-strings on a violin, and then played for the young people to dance, while the mothers and other grave persons conversed in another room." The

EARLY MUSIC

Marquis does not miss the piano-forte, which had been first manufactured in Europe about the middle of the century. Even in Philadelphia they were then known. The first piano in America was made by John Behrent, on Third Street below Brown. He advertised in 1775 that he had "just finished an extraordinary instrument, by the name of the Piano-Forte, made of mahogany, being of the nature of a Harpsichord, with hammers and several changes." Other makers followed. Prominent was Charles Taws, a Scotchman, next the corner of Third and Union Streets, where he began manufacturing about 1787. But the most important of all was an Englishman, Thomas Loud Evenden, who came to the city about 1810, and manufactured piano-fortes, in partnership with Joshua Baker, at 130 Vine Street. Later he carried on business on Fifth Street, where his son and namesake, of whom we shall hear more, taught piano-playing. They seemed to have first found the advertising key-note of later piano-makers. In 1816 they advertised that they "furnished pianos much better in workmanship than even the London pianos." They "confidently challenged any huckster in the city who had the arrogance to call himself an importer to disprove the assertion." A few years afterwards, for some reason, the members of the Evenden family dropped the final name. Loud's pianos became very popular. Thomas Loud, the younger, was one of the principal musicians of Philadelphia.

Before we leave the eighteenth century and its instruments, we must not omit an episode, which, by curious chance, connects our history at once with Philadelphia's tutelary personage and with one of the great English prose-writers. Armstrong, in his "Record of the Opera," makes mention of Benjamin Franklin as one of the earliest amateur musicians in Philadelphia. "He is accredited with the invention of the Harmonica or Musical Glasses. He certainly made them available." The story is that Franklin concealed his harmonica from his wife until it was fit to play, and then woke her with it one night, when she thought it was the music of angels. These musical glasses, played on with moistened fingers, were a favorite musical toy at one time. They were never more than a curiosity. The construction of Franklin's glasses is described in his letters. Franklin also played the guitar. Leigh Hunt, in his autobiography, writes of his mother, who was the daughter of Stephen

EARLY MUSIC

Shewell, a merchant of Philadelphia, and "a vehement man both in public and in family matters." Franklin and Thomas Paine visited at the Shewells'. "My mother," Leigh Hunt writes, "had no accomplishments but the two best of all— a love of nature and of books. Dr. Franklin offered to teach her the guitar, but she was too bashful to become his pupil. She regretted this afterward, partly, no doubt, for having missed so illustrious a master. Her first child, who died, was named after him." He then tells the story of Franklin's harmonica.

Most of the leading men in music had come from Great Britain. Generally they settled first into the more purely commercial lines of manufacture and publishing. Probably the first music-store in the city was Benjamin Carr's "Music Repository." Carr stands out as the most vigorous force for the best musical culture in his day. In his circle were men like George Schetky, Charles P. Hupfeld, and Raynor Taylor. Coming to Philadelphia in 1793, after a thorough musical education under the first church-musicians in England, a man of breeding and of broad culture, joining his efforts with those of Hupfeld, who brought the best German traditions in early boy-

MUSIC IN PHILADELPHIA

hood, Carr and his group started the movement which gave to Philadelphia so striking a musical development in those days, when both the country and the art were in their infancy. The impression which he made upon his associates is proven by the monument erected in St. Peter's Church. The inscription speaks far more directly than the customary language of colleagues,—

BENJAMIN CARR,

A DISTINGUISHED PROFESSOR OF MUSIC,
DIED MAY 24, 1831, AGED 62 YEARS.
CHARITABLE, WITHOUT OSTENTATION,
FAITHFUL AND TRUE IN HIS FRIENDSHIPS,
WITH THE INTELLIGENCE OF A MAN
HE UNITED THE SIMPLICITY OF A CHILD.
IN TESTIMONY OF THE HIGH ESTEEM IN WHICH HE
WAS HELD, THIS MONUMENT IS ERECTED BY
HIS FRIENDS AND ASSOCIATES OF THE
MUSICAL FUND SOCIETY
OF PHILADELPHIA.

The monument was designed by William Strickland, and executed by William Struthers. The first portrait for the Society, that of Mr. Carr, was painted by J. C. Darley in 1831. Of his activity outside of his sphere in the church-service, in which he was pre-eminent, we shall speak later.

Hupfeld, who came from another region

EARLY MUSIC

of Europe, brought his stimulating traditions from a different quarter of the field of music. He it was who inspired his friends, both amateur and professional, with the delights of string-quartette practice, that ideal form of German home music which seems to typify the simple geniality of German family-life. These meetings of Hupfeld's friends were undoubtedly the direct cause of the successful organization which followed.

Thomas Loud has been mentioned. He came to Philadelphia in 1812, and finished his musical apprenticeship under a distinguished teacher, George Pfeffer. It is told that a rivalry arose between teacher and pupil, and a public trial of skill on the piano was arranged. Each performer was to select his piece. Mr. Loud played so finely that his reputation was at once established. His principal field of activity, besides organ-playing, was the conducting of choruses.

The Nestor of this group was Raynor Taylor. Although associated with the stage of English opera and of even lighter programmes, he seems to have taken a prominent position upon his arrival in Philadelphia in 1793, when he was not far from fifty years old. A monument in St. Peter's church-yard tells us that he was

MUSIC IN PHILADELPHIA

"many years organist at St. Peter's Church." An anecdote of his boyhood links us with one of the patriarchs of the art. He used to relate that when he was choir-boy at the King's Chapel (1749–1760), he attended Händel's funeral (April 27, 1759), and that "on this solemn and memorable occasion his hat accidentally fell into the grave and was buried with the remains of that wonderful composer." "Never mind," said some one to whom he told the story, "he left you some of his brains in return." All of which would certainly be a more striking story if Taylor had chanced to be a Mendelssohn.

The youngest of the group, who is still well remembered, thus completes a long line of musical traditions. Benjamin Cross was born in Philadelphia in 1786, of Scotch descent. A graduate of the University of Pennsylvania, he chose his profession against the original wishes of his parents, who wanted him to study medicine. His musical teachers and close associates were Raynor Taylor and Benjamin Carr. Cross transmitted from these men their traditions of musicianship and manhood. His sphere was a broad one. He is said to have sung with distinguished success the barytone part in the oratorios of Händel and of Haydn.

EARLY MUSIC

He taught singing and piano-playing with striking results. But, above all, the monument in the minutes of the Society, whose history we shall presently follow, speaks of his work as vocal conductor. It acknowledges to him a peculiar debt for the foundation of the prosperity and usefulness of that famous Society. His portrait was painted for the Society by Thomas Sully in 1861.

We have made passing mention of George Schetky, a Scotchman, who deserves emphasis as an equal factor in the work of organizing the musical forces of Philadelphia early in the new century. He came as a boy in 1792, to live with his uncle, Alexander Reinagle, but he returned home after a short stay. On his second arrival he soon achieved high standing as a "professor of music." Of the seminaries in which he taught, perhaps the most important was that of Madame Rivardi, in the "Gothic Mansion," on Chestnut Street near Thirteenth. One of his favorite pupils was the late Mrs. Edward Shippen Burd. During this period he lived with Benjamin Carr in closest intimacy; together with a younger musician, Joseph C. Taws, they kept a bachelor's house. After a third absence in Scotland, he married, in 1823, one of his pupils, Elizabeth M. Paterson, of Philadelphia. The Musical Fund Society likewise erected a monument to him in St. Peter's church-yard, and had his portrait painted by J. C. Darley. His widow survived him until 1888.

In leaving the eighteenth century, we must confess that until its close music received little encouragement from the public. It was principally limited to the churches and to the small circles which grouped about the few resident musicians. But with the beginning of the new century there appears a decided impulse towards the formation of musical societies, mainly for the performance of the great vocal masterpieces. The old Uranian Society was founded in 1787 for the improvement of church music. It continued until after 1800, meeting at the corner of Third and Market Streets. The Harmonic Society, formed in 1802 for a similar purpose, aspired nevertheless to concerts, and usually gave at least one every year. Some of the places of performance were the Second Presbyterian Church, at Third and Arch Streets, and the Hall of the University, on Fourth Street below Arch. The Haydn Society, instituted in 1809, consisted in 1819 of eighty ladies and fifty gentlemen. The managers were the Rev. John Goodman,

EARLY MUSIC

Joseph George, and George Emerick. One announcement tells that "the object of the Society has been for many years to introduce and improve themselves in psalmody." They might have added the study of rhetoric.

Probably of more importance was the Handelian Society, which gave some famous concerts, one of which, at the Tabernacle Church in 1815, yielded for the benefit of the poor the sum of $1017.95, a sum which seems colossal even to the Philadelphian musicians of to-day. It would not be too bold a venture to assert that no local concert has since surpassed this achievement.

In 1817 a small choir was started in the Rev. Thomas N. Skinner's church, known as the Fifth Presbyterian, then on Locust Street, west of Eighth, where now is Musical Fund Hall. There was some difficulty, as choirs were unknown in the Presbyterian Church. Other societies were the Harmonic, of St. John's English Lutheran Church, meeting in 1819 at the corner of Sixth and Race Streets. At the same time the Independent Harmonic Society, of which Joseph McIlhenny was president, met at Fourth and Vine Streets. Finally, there was the Union Harmonic Society, of

MUSIC IN PHILADELPHIA

the same period, in the rooms of the old Harmonic, in Norris' Alley; James Weir was the president. The St. Cecilia Society, established in 1824, had its hall on South Fourth Street. The first president was John Neagle, the artist. He was succeeded in 1825 by Colonel Andrew M. Prevost. The leader was Edward R. Hansen; Thomas Carr was vocal conductor.

One of the greatest musical occasions was the performance of selections from the "Messiah" and from the "Creation" at St. Augustine's Church, in June, 1810, with an orchestra of fifty performers.

All these forces, struggling for organized musical activity, were finally crystallized in one society, which in turn reacted with strong impetus and with a greatly improved standard on the musical life of the city.

EARLY MUSIC

CHAPTER IV. BEGINNINGS OF THE MUSICAL FUND SOCIETY.

THERE is no doubt that most events of moment to the world began without flourish of trumpets, in ignorance of their significance. Nay, it might be said that it is in this unconsciousness that lies the strength of the movement.

For several years previous to 1820, a small circle of lovers of music were in the habit of meeting during the winter months on Wednesday evenings at their houses for musical enjoyment and cultivation. Among these were Dr. William P. De Wees, Dr. Robert M. Patterson, John K. Kane, Leonard Koecker, Peter S. Duponceau, Charles A. Poulson, and others. The best musicians were invited, and chosen friends who appreciated the quartettes of "Beethoven, Boccherini, and other composers." Let us hope these included Haydn and Mozart. The musicians were Charles F. Hupfeld, leader, John Hupfeld, second violin and sometimes tenor (or viola), P. Gilles and

MUSIC IN PHILADELPHIA

George Schetky, violoncellos. Occasional violinists were John C. Hommann and his two sons, John and Charles, and Dr. Rêné La Roche.

Charles Hupfeld, in 1816, tried to establish with Benjamin Carr, P. Gilles, and others, a society for regular practice. They met at Earle and Sully's gallery of paintings, at the house next to the northwest corner of Fifth and Chestnut Streets. But they found it difficult to keep a sufficient number of players together. Gradually to the study of concerted music was added the distinct purpose of a fund for the relief of musicians.

This subject was frequently discussed at the quartette parties; and at length a public meeting was held by a number of gentlemen, professional and amateur, on Friday evening, January 7, 1820, in the front room of the second story of Elliott's hotel on Chestnut Street, next door to Peter S. Duponceau's residence, at the northeast corner of Sixth and Chestnut Streets. Among those present were Dr. William P. De Wees, Dr. Robert M. Patterson, Joseph Fisher, Benjamin Carr, George Schetky, P. Gilles, the Messrs. Hommann, Charles F. Hupfeld and his brother John, Thomas Loud, John K. Kane, and Charles A. Poulson. Dr. De Wees presided, and Mr.

EARLY MUSIC

Kane acted as secretary. The meeting deemed it expedient that a society should be instituted for the purpose of providing a fund for the relief and support of decayed musicians and their families. A committee to draft a constitution was appointed, consisting of Messrs. Carr, Charles Hupfeld, Cross, and Dr. Patterson. At a late meeting another committee, comprising most of the last mentioned, was appointed to receive nominations for membership in the proposed society. All the committees consisted, for the most part, of professional musicians. At a special meeting, on February 3, the report of the former committee was unanimously adopted as the constitution of the Musical Fund Society of Philadelphia. On the 29th of the same month a meeting for the election of officers was held at Elliott's Hotel, which resulted as follows:

    Dr. William P. De Wees - President.
    Dr. Robert M. Patterson - Vice-President.
    Daniel Lammot - - - Treasurer.
    John K. Kane - - - Secretary.

Managers of the Fund.—James W. Barker, Thomas Artley, Francis G. Smith, Edward Hudson, Benjamin Carr, William Strickland, Henry P. Barrekens, William Hawkins, Charles A. Poulson, Benjamin Say, George Schetky, and Andrew Farrouihl.

MUSIC IN PHILADELPHIA

Directors of Music.—Raynor Taylor, Benjamin Carr, C. F. Hupfeld, P. Gilles, Benjamin Cross, M. E. Brenan, Thomas Sully, I. Le Folle, I. T. David, George Schetky, Charles I. Nicholas, and J. C. Hommann.

The following eighty-five names were reported to be members of the Society:

Thomas Artley.
Allyn Bach.
John Brown.
H. P. Barrekens.
Geo. E. Blake.
Wm. C. Beck.
M. E. Brenan.
C. I. Brown.
Jas. H. Barker.
Dr. John Barnes.
Lewis F. Bernhart.
Ben. Carr.
Ben. Cross.
Jacob Churr, Jr.
Isaac P. Cole.
Ben. S. Clemens.
G. Carusi.
S. Carusi.
L. Carusi.
Geo. Campbell.
Dr. Wm. P. De Wees.
I. T. David.
Tobias W. Durney.
Elijah Dallett.
F. Eberlé
Jos. Fisher.

Henry G. Freeman.
I. L. Frederick.
Daniel C. Freytag.
A. Farrouihl.
John Fowle, Jr.
John Fury.
P. Gilles.
John F. Greland.
John Graham.
T. Greland.
Wm. Gallager.
C. F. Hupfeld.
John Hupfeld.
J. C. Hommann.
J. C. Hommann, Jr.
Wm. Hawkins.
Ed. Hudson.
Thos. Hopkins.
Wm. Harrison.
Francis Hopkinson.
Jas. Henderson.
Abram L. Hart.
Dr. Wm. E. Horner.
John K. Kane.
J. G. Klemm.
Leonard Koecker.

EARLY MUSIC

John Keating, Jr.	Chas. F. Roberts.
Thos. Loud.	Thos. Sully.
I. Le Folle.	Geo. Schetky.
Daniel Lammot.	F. G. Smith.
Rêné La Roche, Jr.	R. S. Smith.
Jacob Lex.	Wm. Strickland.
G. Marshall.	David Sergeant.
Wm. McIlhenny, Jr.	John Sidebotham.
Chas. I. Nicholas.	Gurney Smith.
Philip N. Nicklin.	Benjamin Say.
Chas. Penneweyre.	Robt. W. Sykes.
P. Perdriaux.	Jos. C. Taws.
Chas. A. Poulson.	Raynor Taylor.
Dr. Robt. M. Patterson.	John Wheeler.
Thos. N. Palmer.	Geo. F. Womrath.
Thos. P. Roberts.	

Note.—David Sergeant declined, leaving the number eighty-four.

Many of the most distinguished citizens early became members of the Society and took an active interest in its advancement and work.

The relief of musicians, apparently the original prime object, seems in reality to have been rather an excuse,—that which might give the society a surviving cause, after the special circle of incorporating members had departed. The title and the term "decayed musicians" was undoubtedly suggested by that of the London Musical Fund Society, which was in existence at that time.

MUSIC IN PHILADELPHIA

The fact that the beneficial purpose appears foremost in all the formal documents, in the title, the legend, the stated object of the first meeting, and the act of incorporation, is not convincing. According to the annual report of May 3, 1831, "the primary object . . . was to reform the state of neglect into which the beautiful art of music had fallen. The secondary object in the formation of the Society was the provision of a fund for relieving decayed musicians. This was a graft on the first project; but its value was so highly appreciated that in the arrangement of the constitution it was assigned the highest rank." The driving motive in the whole undertaking was, without doubt, a high ambition, far beyond that of any existing musical association. It was intended to advance music to the highest point, and to present to the public the finest compositions, both sacred and secular. But in the linking of its twin objects, it was probably unique in this country. Perhaps it was a suggestion of the old verse, that

"Music, like mercy, is twice blessed,—
It blesseth him that gives and him that takes."

The early meetings of the directors were held at the residence of Benjamin Carr, at 7 Powell Street, between Fifth and Sixth;

EARLY MUSIC

once at George Schetky's, at 71 Locust Street. At one of them there were elected, as conductors of instrumental music, C. F. Hupfeld, P. Gilles, and George Schetky; as conductors of vocal music, L. F. Bernhart, Thomas Loud, and M. E. Brenan. The curators were J. B. De Bree, T. M. Durney, Thomas N. Palmer, and F. Gurney Smith. It was agreed that the practising should be held on Thursday evenings of each week during the year, excepting the months of June, July, and August, alternately with vocal and instrumental music. The first of these practisings were held in the third-story room of the building No. 118 Chestnut Street, on the southwest corner of Carpenters' Court; afterwards at Carpenters' Hall, when that building was rented by the Society.

The board of managers held their first meeting on the 7th of March, at the house of the treasurer, Daniel Lammot, at 98 S. Front Street. Subsequently, until a room was rented, they met at Thomas Astley's, on the southwest corner of Eighth and Walnut.

An amusing correspondence between the first secretary and two members-elect is actually preserved in the original writing. The first letter, written jointly by ≡≡ H.

MUSIC IN PHILADELPHIA

and 𝅘𝅥 H., whom we discover in James or "Gimmy" Henderson and Francis Hopkinson, is an elaborate structure of puns and plays, none of which we can escape, as they are faithfully underlined with unctuous gusto. So absolute is the determination to import all phrases and words which remotely bear on musical terms, that the actual sense of the letter lapses into an obscure background. They complain of a bass viol-ation of the freedom of speech; they are intent on putting a stop to such high-toned infractions. They threaten to flagellate the secretary and make him shake. They tell him he will meet with an insurmountable bar in the fiddel-ity of their souls, and much other innocent nonsense. They underscore every appearance of "voices," "time," "seconds." Finally they subscribe themselves: "Hoping you may continue *con gracio* always *affetuoso* and without variation a *trio* of friends until the grand *finale*." The answer of the secretary, who easily vanquishes his adversaries on their chosen ground, is quite worth quoting in full.

"To Messieurs 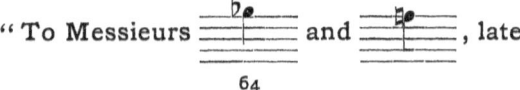 , late

EARLY MUSIC

members-elect of the Musical Fund Society
of Philadelphia,—

1.

"*Hautbois!* and did you think to *beat*,
　By puns of neither point nor fire,
In a *short note* of half a sheet,
　Those who have often *filled a choir?*

2.

"You've *strained* your wits exceeding much,
　Have *marked your time* and *struck* your *blow*,
But *vile in* every thing you touch,
　Your vileness never sunk *solo*.

3.

"Your threats I value not a dime;
　For well does *shaking* Gimmy know
That *hymn* I've *struck full* many a *time*,
　But he dared never *give a blow*.

4.

"Yet you of *flageoletting* prate,
　As though you n'er had tried the game,
Nor felt, ye Gadshill knaves, the weight
　Of my much punned and dreaded name.

5.

"Ye *quavering* fools, who do not know
　A psalm tune from a country dance,—
Truly, we weep to mark your low
　And-ante Christian ignorance.

MUSIC IN PHILADELPHIA

6.

"For you *bass trumpets* are the thing,
    Fitted to make a braying sound;
That whether you do *play* or *sing*,
    Your native *notes* may still *resound*.

7.

"'Twill not *seem funny* to you then
    That we your *concert* should despise,
Nor wish for *harmony* with men
    Who harmony can never prize.

8.

"Your scornful puns, ye *harp*-y pair,
    We men of *note* with scorn repay:—
Ye members true of *discord's bar*,
    We *drum* you from our *bar* away.

      "Signed and Sealed with the Society Seal."

"Feb. 27, 1820."

At one of the preliminary meetings the members were distinguished as professional and amateur. The former were:

L. F. Bernhart.	B. Carr.
A. Bacon.	J. Churr, Jr.
G. E. Blake.	I. P. Cole.
M. E. Brenan.	J. B. DeBree.
G. Carusi.	F. E. Eberlé
S. Carusi.	I. L. Frederick.
L. Carusi.	J. Fuss.

EARLY MUSIC

A. Farrouihl.	A. L. Hart.
P. Gilles.	J. G. Klemm.
T. Greland.	T. Loud.
C. F. Hupfeld.	I. Le Folle.
J. Hupfeld.	J. Sidebotham.
T. Hopkins.	J. C. Taws.
J. C. Hommann.	R. Taylor.
J. C. Hommann, Jr.	J. Wheeler.

A committee was appointed to wait on such ladies as they might select, and solicit them to become members of the Society.*

On the 29th of March a committee reported that they had contracted with John Lavel for a third-story room at No. 118 Chestnut Street, on the southwest corner of Carpenters' Court, at a rent of one hundred and fifty dollars for one year. From the minutes it appears that before this lease some meetings were held at Elliott's Hotel, others at the house of Dr. De Wees, the president, at No. 154 Chestnut Street.

Committees on finance and on distribution were appointed on April 19, and at the same meeting the by-laws were adopted. One of the articles provided, in order the more effectually to promote the benevolent aim of the institution, that the board elect

---

* The members elected after incorporation will be found enrolled in the appendix.

annually two physicians, and that the latter visit, at the request of the Committee on Distribution, such members and their families as may require medical advice or assistance, and in all cases prescribe gratuitously. At the first annual meeting of the Society, held at the hall, No. 118 Chestnut Street, on May 2, 1820, substantially the same officers were elected. Francis G. Smith appears as treasurer.

Much difficulty existed in obtaining copies of parts in preparation for the first concert of the Society. A letter from Peters, in Leipzig, said that he was unable to fill the order in its entirety. To procure the instrumental parts of Beethoven's "Hallelujah Chorus" from "The Mount of Olives," one of the members visited New York. Mr. Gillingham was paid five dollars for making copies of parts belonging to the Händel and Haydn Society of New York.

It was intended to give Haydn's "Creation" at the first concert, but the music could not be procured, either from abroad or from Baltimore, New York, or Boston. Much time had been spent in rehearsing the oratorio.

The following is the notice as published in the newspapers relating to the preparations for the first concert:

EARLY MUSIC

"MUSICAL FUND SOCIETY
OF PHILADELPHIA.

"The performing members of the Society and all others concerned are respectfully requested to give their punctual attendance at the appointed Rehearsals as preparatory to the First Concert for the Benefit of the Fund, to be held at the Grand Saloon, Washington Hall, on Tuesday, 24th inst. [April], viz. :

"1st. On Tuesday evening, 17th instant, a Vocal and Instrumental Rehearsal for Performing Members only, at the Hall of the Society, lately occupied by the Bank of the United States, Carpenters' Court, precisely at 7 o'clock.

"2d. On Thursday evening, 19th instant, at 7 o'clock precisely, at the Society's Hall, a stated practising of the Sinfonias, Overtures, Concerts, &c., at which the Members of the Society may attend.

"3d. On Monday, 23d instant, at 2 o'clock in the afternoon, the Grand Saloon, Washington Hall, a General Rehearsal of the Concert, at which the Members of the Society, not engaged in the performances, are invited to attend.

"N.B.—In order to avoid confusion or intrusion, the Members of the Society are requested to show their tickets of Membership to the doorkeepers or janitor. Those Ladies and Gentlemen who have kindly volunteered their assistance on this occasion will be presented with tickets of admission on Tuesday, 17th instant, at the Hall of the Society, which tickets they also will have the goodness to show to the doorkeepers or janitor, at every succeeding Rehearsal or Practising.

"By order of the Board of Directors of the Music.

"G. SCHETKY,
"April 16, 1821."   Secretary.

MUSIC IN PHILADELPHIA

"MUSICAL FUND SOCIETY
OF PHILADELPHIA.

"The public are respectfully informed, that the First Concert, for the benefit of the Fund, will be repeated on Tuesday, 8th May, 1821, at the Grand Saloon, Washington Hall, with the addition of some Vocal Solos, &c.

"The Members of the Society will please to apply at the Society's Hall, in Carpenters' Court, for their two Ladies' Tickets, on Saturday, Monday, and Tuesday, from 9 till 1 o'clock."

The first concert of the Society was given on Tuesday, April 24, 1821, at Washington Hall, on Third Street, near Spruce. A programme has been most happily preserved of its second performance, of which the wording follows; a reduced fac-simile of the first page is also given. In regard to this repetition, a minute of a late meeting records a vote that it "should not be considered as one of the two concerts . . . authorized to be given this year."

SECOND PERFORMANCE
of the
FIRST CONCERT
for the benefit of the
MUSICAL FUND SOCIETY
OF PHILADELPHIA,

SECOND PERFORMANCE

OF THE

FIRST CONCERT

FOR THE BENEFIT OF THE

MUSICAL FUND SOCIETY

OF PHILADELPHIA.

TUESDAY, MAY 8, 1821.

At the Grand Saloon, Washington Hall.

With the addition of some *VOCAL SOLOS.*

Conductors—Messrs. B. Carr, B. Cross, P. Gilles, C. F. Hupfeld, T. Loud, G. Schetky.

PLAN OF THE CONCERT

PART FIRST.

Grand Sinfonia in E.   Romberg

Vocal Duett, "The Butterfly,"   Sale

> Gay Being, born to flutter thro' the day,
>   Sport in the sunshine of the present hour,
> On the sweet rose thy painted wings display,
>   And cull the fragrance of the op'ning flower!
>
> Time hastens on; the summer ends too soon;
>   Take then the rosy minutes as they fly;
> For soon, alas, your little life is gone,
>   To-day you sparkle, and to-morrow die.

Concerto Violoncello----Mr. Gilles, from B. Romberg's Concerto in D., followed by an air with variations, composed by Mr. Gilles

Air, vocal, "Donald,"   Original Scottish Melody

> When first you courted me, I own,
>   I fondly favoured you;
> Apparent worth and high renown
>   Made me believe you true, Donald.

EARLY MUSIC

Tuesday, May 8, 1821,
At the Grand Saloon, Washington Hall,
With the addition of some
Vocal Solos.

Conductors.—Messrs. B. Carr, B. Cross, P. Gilles, C. F. Hupfeld, T. Loud, G. Schetky.

PLAN OF THE CONCERT.

PART FIRST.

Grand Sinfonia in E.   Romberg
Vocal Duett, "The Butterfly"   Sale

> Gay being, born to flutter thro' the day,
>   Sport in the sunshine of the present hour,
> On the sweet rose thy painted wings display,
>   And cull the fragrance of the op'ning flower!
>
> Time hastens on; the summer ends too soon;
>   Take then the rosy minutes as they fly;
> For soon, alas, your little life is gone,
>   To-day you sparkle, and to-morrow die.

Concerto Violoncello—Mr. Gilles, from B. Romberg's Concerto in D, followed by an air with variations, composed by   Mr. Gilles
Air, vocal, "Donald"   Original Scottish Melody

> When first you courted me, I own,
>   I fondly favoured you;
> Apparent worth and high renown
>   Made me believe you true, Donald.

MUSIC IN PHILADELPHIA

> Each virtue then seem'd to adorn
>   The man esteem'd by me;
> But, now the mask's thrown off, I scorn
>   To waste one thought on thee, Donald.
>
> O then for ever haste away,
>   Away from love and me!
> Go seek a heart that's like your own,
>   And come no more to me, Donald.
> For I'll reserve myself alone
>   For one that's more like me;
> If such a one I cannot find,
>   I'll fly from love and thee, Donald.

Overture—Dell Opera Tancredi	Rossini
Glee and Chorus—Awake, Æolian Lyre, with orchestra accompaniments by B. Carr	Danby

Glee and Chorus.

> Awake, Æolian Lyre, awake!
> And give to rapture all thy trembling strings:
> From Helicon's harmonious springs,
> A thousand rills their mazy progress take.
>
> The laughing flow'rs that round them blow,
> Drink life and fragrance as they flow.
> Now the rich stream of music winds along,
> Deep, majestic, smooth, and strong,
>
> Thro' verdant vales and Ceres' golden reign;
> Now rolling down the steep amain,
> Headlong, impetuous, see it pour,
> The rocks and nodding groves rebellow to the roar.

EARLY MUSIC

PART SECOND.

Concerto Violin, Mr. Hupfeld   Rode
Polacca, "Trifler, Forbear"   Bishop

Recit.
> Trifler, forbear; deceit in flattery lies;
> We may endure it, but we must despise.

Air.
> Go, trifler, go; your flattery leave,
>   That lure which leads our sex astray!
> Still smiling only to deceive,
>   And more securely to betray!
>
> On Etna's side thus verdure bright
>   Deludes the swain, and hope inspires;
> While, with an overwhelming night
>   The dread Volcano pours its fires!
>   Trifler, forbear!
>
> Go, trifler, go, &c.

Grand Sinfonia in C   Beethoven
New Glee and Chorus—Sequel to
  the "Red Cross Knight," with
  orchestra accompaniments by
  B. Carr   Dr. Clarke

SEQUEL TO THE RED CROSS KNIGHT.

Solo, Bass Voice.
> I cannot stay, cried the Red Cross Knight,
> Nor can I feast with thee:
> But I must haste to a pleasant bow'r,
> Where a lady's waiting for me.

MUSIC IN PHILADELPHIA

Trio.

>Oh, say not so, dear Red Cross Knight,
>Nor heed that fond lady,
>For she can't compare with my daughter so fair,
>And she shall attend on thee.

Solo, Bass Voice.

>Now must I go, cried the Red Cross Knight,
>For that lady I'm to wed,
>And the feast guests and bridemaids all are met,
>And prepared the bridal bed.

Trio.

>Now nay, now nay, thou Red Cross Knight,
>My daughter shall wed with thee,
>And the mass shall be sung,
>And the bells shall be rung,
>And we'll feast right merrily.

Chorus.

>And the mass shall be sung,
>And the bells shall be rung,
>And we'll feast right merrily.

Trio.

>And as the lady prest the Knight,
>With her ladies clad in pall,
>Oh then bespake a pilgrim boy,
>As he stood in the hall.

Solo, Treble Voice.

>Now Heav'n thee save, Sir Red Cross Knight,
>I'm come from the North country,
>Where a lady is laid all on her death bed,
>And evermore calls for thee.

EARLY MUSIC

Solo, Bass Voice.

    Alas! alas! thou pilgrim boy,
    Sad news thou tellest me,
    Now must I ride full hastily,
    To comfort that dear lady.

Treble Voices.

    Oh heed him not, the ladies cried,
    But send a page to see.

Trio and Chorus.

    While the mass is sung,
    And the bells are rung,
    And we feast merrily.

Solo, Treble Voice.

    Again bespake the pilgrim boy:
    Ye need not send to see,
    For, know, Sir Knight, that lady's dead,
    And died for love of thee.

Trio.

    Oh! then the Red Cross Knight was pale,
    And not a word could say;
    But his heart did swell, and his tears down fell,
    And he almost swoon'd away.
    And where is her grave, said the Red Cross Knight,
    The grave where she doth lay?
    Oh, I know well, cried the pilgrim boy,
    And I'll shew thee the way.
    The Knight was sad, the pilgrim sigh'd,

Solo, Treble Voice.

    While the Warder loud did cry,
    Let the mass be sung,
    And the bells be rung,
    And the feast eat merrily.

MUSIC IN PHILADELPHIA

Trio and Chorus.
> Let the mass be sung,
> And the bells be rung,
> And the feast eat merrily.

Overture—De L'Opera Les Deux Aveugles De Toledo, full orchestra   Mehul

LEADER—MR. C. F. HUPFELD.

Principal violins—Messrs. De Luce, Heinrich, Kahn, Getze, &c., &c. Principal violoncello—M. P. Gilles. Violoncellos—Messrs. Hommann, senr., &c. Tenors—Messrs. Cantor, C. Hommann, &c. Principal double bass—Mr. Schetky. Double basses—Messrs. J. Hommann and Klemm. Principal flute—Mr. Dannenberg. Principal bassoon—Mr. J. D. Weisse, from Bethlehem.

The CONDUCTORS of the VOCAL Music will alternately preside at the ORGAN.

The Orchestra will consist of one hundred Vocal and Instrumental performers.

TO COMMENCE AT 7 O'CLOCK.

At a meeting of the board of managers on April 30, Dr. William P. De Wees, Benjamin Carr, and William T. Birch were elected trustees, "in whom shall be vested

EARLY MUSIC

all the estate and effects, now and which may belong to the Society, and in whose names all future investments of the funds shall be made, and execute all contracts for the benefit of the Society."

With all the magnificent progress we have traced, there was still a goodly remnant of old prejudice. A suspicious taint still clung to the professional musician. At a meeting in May, 1820, it was resolved, "That no female professional members be admitted without a written certificate from some lady of established character in this city."

In the same year we find a bill of sixteen dollars and sixty-three cents for candles approved by the board. Gas, it seems, was still an experiment at this time.

MUSIC IN PHILADELPHIA

CHAPTER V. EARLY YEARS OF THE MUSICAL FUND SOCIETY.

IN May, 1821, it was decided that the oratorio of the "Creation" be prepared for the next concert.

A little later a lease was concluded with the Carpenters' Society for their hall, at a rent of three hundred dollars a year. Alterations were directed to be made at an expense not exceeding fifteen dollars. It is not so strange to find in the treasurer's quarterly report, in July, the promising balance of eleven hundred and sixty-eight dollars and twenty-seven cents. A more prodigal spirit led, in January of the next year, to the provision of refreshments "for the performing members at practisings and private rehearsals, under such regulations as may be deemed proper, the expenses not to exceed two dollars."

In preparation for the "Creation," the instrumental parts were borrowed of the Moravian Brethren at Bethlehem. In February a committee, consisting of "other than professional members," was appointed "to procure an accession of Ladies and Gentlemen to the vocal rehearsals."

MUSICAL FUND SOCIETY

The performance of an oratorio was something of a Herculean achievement in those days. The honor of first producing Haydn's "Creation" in the United States belongs to the Moravians of Bethlehem, where it was given in 1811. The copies, made from the score of Peters, are still preserved. The Händel and Haydn Society of Boston gave the first complete performance of the oratorio in 1819.

Too many difficulties there must have been; for, instead of the oratorio, we find this to be the programme:

THE SECOND CONCERT

For the Benefit of the

MUSICAL FUND SOCIETY

OF PHILADELPHIA

will be given on Tuesday Evening, March 19th, 1822,
at the Grand Saloon, Washington Hall,
commencing at 7 o'clock precisely.

Mrs. Burke and Mr. Phillips have politely offered their
assistance on this occasion.

LEADER, MR. HUPFELD.

PART I.

Sinfonia	Full Band	Romberg.
Song	Mr. Phillips "Gentle Airs"	
	from the Oratorio of Athalia.	

MUSIC IN PHILADELPHIA

Violoncello obligato   Mr. Gilles   Haendel.
Duet   Mrs. Burke and Mr. Phillips "I love thee" Bishop.
Overture to Sophronista   Paer.

PART II.

Concerto for Violin   Mr. Hupfeld   Franzl.
Song   Mr. Phillips.
Variations on "Robin Adair" for Violoncello.
       P. Gilles, composed for the
             Musical Fund Society   P. Gilles.
Overture to Demophon   Vogel.
Polacca   Mrs. Burke "Soldiers' Rest"   Clifton.
Finale   Full Band.

Tickets for the Concert are for sale at G. E. Blake's, 13 South 5th Street, at Bacon & Hart's, No. 11 South 4th St., at Willig's, No. 171 Chestnut Street, and Carey & Lea's, corner Chestnut and Fourth streets.

Members are requested to call for their Ladies' tickets at the Hall of the Society on Carpenters' Court, on Monday between 10 and 2, and on Tuesday between 10 & 5 o'clock.

It was still the old-fashioned kind of concert of the first years of the century,—a mass of ephemeral and local "celebrities" floated by sparse mention of a Händel, a Mozart, and a Paer. But the directors reported a large attendance and a good reception.

Mrs. Burke was the most famous American singer until she was outrivalled by a Mrs. French.

MUSICAL FUND SOCIETY

The 10th of June was finally set for the performance of "The Creation," at Washington Hall. Announcements in the newspapers read as follows:

"ORATORIO
OF THE CREATION OF THE WORLD
BY HAYDN.

"This very celebrated work will be performed by the Musical Fund Society for the first time in this city on Monday next, June 10th, at half past seven o'clock in the evening at the Washington Hall.

"The Society has spared no pains to make this programme as perfect as possible. The parts have been in the course of preparation and rehearsal for several months, and the vocal and instrumental performers will amount to upwards of 100.

"The Society will be generously assisted by many Ladies and Gentlemen not of their number, and among these they have particular pleasure in being able to name Mrs. French.

"A pamphlet has been published, containing the words of the oratorio, with notes and observations on the music, principally selected from the various European authors, who have written on this great composition.

"Tickets One Dollar, and the pamphlet at 12½ cents, may be had at the music stores of Messrs. Blake, Willig, Bacon & Hart, Frederick and George Bacon, No. 66 Chestnut Street; and at the book stores of Messrs. Carey & Lea, A. Small, and of Thomas De Silver, Market Street, of Messrs. Beck & Stewart, and at the Hall on the evening of performance."

MUSIC IN PHILADELPHIA

"MUSICAL FUND SOCIETY.

" The Ladies and Gentlemen engaged in the performance of the Oratorio on Monday Evening are respectfully requested to be in their places at the orchestra at 7 o'clock, as the tuning of the instruments will begin at that time.

" It is the determination of the conductors, that the performance shall commence at the hour appointed, half-past seven."

"MUSICAL FUND SOCIETY.

" The members are informed that a committee will attend at the Society's Hall, in Carpenters' Court, on Thursday, Friday, Saturday, and Monday next, from 10 until 1 o'clock for the distribution of Ladies' Tickets for the approaching oratorio. Those amateur members who have not yet taken their Tickets for the present year will observe that there is due an annual contribution of five dollars."

The title-page of the pamphlet above mentioned is as follows:

THE WORDS OF

the

CREATION OF THE WORLD,

a

SACRED ORATORIO

By Joseph Haydn

as performed by

the

MUSICAL FUND SOCIETY

MUSICAL FUND SOCIETY
of Philadelphia,
at Washington Hall, June 10th, 1822,
with
Notes
Critical and Explanatory, a memoir of Haydn, etc.

Philadelphia
Printed for the Musical Fund Society by T. H. Palmer
1822.

The programme announces as conductors:

Vocal.	Instrumental.
Benjamin Carr	P. Gilles
Benjamin Cross	Chas. F. Hupfeld
Thomas Loud	J. G. Klemm,

as Leader, Mr. Hupfeld.

"Moreover, on this occasion the orchestra will include more than one hundred and twenty performers; and the conductors are happy to inform the society that Mrs. French has politely offered her valuable assistance."

Mrs. French was a pupil of Benjamin Carr. She is highly praised in Dyer's "Collection of Church Music." Her triumph was unquestioned. The newspapers, in their rivalry of homage, frequently "dropped into poetry" over her power. Of all these verses, the following are given some point by the accident of the falling of part of

MUSIC IN PHILADELPHIA

the ceiling at Washington Hall during one of Mrs. French's concerts.

> "'Tis said that Orpheus played so well
> He raised Eurydice from Hell;
> And St. Cecilia sang so clear
> That angels leaned from Heaven to hear.
>
> "But our Cecilia far excels
> These fabled feats. Her trills and swells
> Enchant the vaulted roofs and walls,
> Until the azure ceiling falls."

When it came to rehearsing the "Creation," it was found that the trombone parts could not be filled by musicians of the city. Again the aid of the music-loving Moravians was invoked. Jedediah and Timothy Weiss came down from Bethlehem with another performer, and Jedediah thus describes an occurrence at one of the rehearsals: "I remember well, I played the bass trombone; when the recitative was sung, wherein the creation of the lion was described, we, the trombonists, blew one long note of four quarters. The conductor rapped; all became silent. The part was repeated three times, with the same result. One of the performers in our rear was overheard to say, 'What folly to get country folks to play such important parts without any more practice than a last re-

MUSICAL FUND SOCIETY

hearsal.' The recitative was repeated a fourth time with the same result. We then did not know that they had stopped on our account. Mr. Hupfeld then came and examined our notes, and proclaimed aloud, 'They are right, gentlemen! the basses must hold out four full quarters.' They had played short notes before. The object of the composer was to imitate the lion's roar, which was most effectively done by long notes on brass instruments. After the performance was over, one of the players, a German, remarked to me, 'You blay vell your bart;' to which I replied, 'If they give us nothing more difficult, this is easy enough.' I did not let him know that we had practised our parts thoroughly ere we left home." At the concert, it is related, these trombone players were the objects of the greatest curiosity. Their large brass instruments were a novelty in a Philadelphia orchestra; few had ever seen them before.

Newspaper comments on the great event are doubly interesting: they show the public importance of the concert, and the plane of journalistic criticism. On the whole, too, they reflect best the actual state of public appreciation. "Poulson's Daily Advertiser," of June 10, 1822, says *inter alia:* "So imposing a display of beauty and

MUSIC IN PHILADELPHIA

fashion has seldom been witnessed in this city. According to the general opinion of those who are judges of music of that description, this great piece, never attempted here before, was well got up and finely executed. The more soft, simple, and touching parts were universally admired. We recognized the air and voice of our favorite Mrs. French, with peculiar pleasure in the last duet. A repetition of the performance would equally contribute to the improvement and benefit of the institution, to the diffusion of scientific and sublime music, and to the gratification of the public at large." The audience was reported to number from eighteen hundred to two thousand, "the largest ever known at a musical performance in this city."

One notice, by the naïveté of its comment, tells most directly of the taste of the day. "It was attended by a numerous and respectable company of ladies and gentlemen, who appeared to be more pleased than it was expected they would be. Some, indeed, were heard to say that, 'if they were not fearful of their taste being called into question, they would not be pleased at all,' and it may be supposed that others would have made similar declarations, if they had been equally candid."

MUSICAL FUND SOCIETY

It ought, however, to be recollected that they were unaccustomed to the genus to which the music of this oratorio belongs. Recitatives to any extent were never before introduced at our concerts. Chromatic and enharmonic passages also were but sparingly used, the simple diatonic being found most effective."

The high standard was to be maintained resolutely. The directors voted that the Serenata of "Acis and Galatea," by Händel, be performed at the first concert of the ensuing year, instead of an oratorio. This was not done; however there were constant signs of the strong public spirit of the members of the Society.

In the preceding October, Thomas H. Palmer made an offer to the directors of the use of his organ until the end of the year. Next autumn Dr. Robert M. Patterson presented to the Society three volumes of the "London Quarterly Musical Magazine." At a meeting in the following November the directors of music reported to the Board of Managers that the oratorio of "The Creation" would be ready for performance in three weeks. At this meeting George Schetky gave the use of his organ for the approaching occasion. Benjamin Carr offers the loan of his piano at a meeting in 1823 "for the ensuing concert."

The best test of the success of the oratorio concert was its repetition in November of the same year in answer to a universal wish.

The general opinion in which the young Society was held is shown by various propositions made by established institutions. They concerned the question of a concert hall, which was the absorbing problem. The first concerts had been given at Washington Hall, in the "Grand Saloon," on Third Street above Spruce. This building seems to have resembled, in its general plan, the hall built by the Society. It was probably the favorite resort for concerts and balls. In March, 1823, Washington Hall* was burned to the ground. Although this event put the Society in some straits, it undoubtedly hastened, if it did not cause, the enterprise which completed its establishment in giving it a home. On the 22d of March of this year, a meeting of the board was held, at which, among other things, a committee reported a certificate of an act of the legislature, incorporating

---

* Strictly the hall of the Washington Benevolent Society.

MUSICAL FUND SOCIETY

the Musical Fund Society of Philadelphia. At this meeting there was appointed a committee to inquire into the expediency of building a hall for the Society. The necessity was urgent. The only hall which could be used for concerts was the Chestnut Street Theatre, near Fifth Street, for which the rent of an evening was at that time two hundred dollars. The theatre was, in fact, engaged for the next concert, which was given in April, 1823, with this announcement:

The Third Miscellaneous
CONCERT
of the Musical Fund Society of
Philadelphia
will be given at the New Theatre on Thursday
evening the 24th inst.
Leader, Mr. Hupfeld.

Then follows the programme, of which the first number was Mozart's overture to "Figaro." Further down is a chorus of Mozart used for words on the landing of Columbus. There is a Haydn Sinfonia, which was certainly not a symphony. The rest is made up of concertos for violin and for violoncello, and of songs by English composers; the day of the Italians had not yet come. But the report in May showed a large gain from concerts.

MUSIC IN PHILADELPHIA

In this connection it may be mentioned that the first case of relief was favorably reported at the stated meeting on July 1. In recommending a pension of two hundred dollars a year to one highly distinguished in his profession, the committee could not "withhold an expression of satisfaction that so conspicuous a proof of the usefulness of our institution has been presented by the incident, and that the honor has been reserved for the Society, of comforting the age and relieving the distress of one of the first and most honored among the professional men of our country."

The question of a permanent hall was still unsolved. There was a thought of holding the concerts exclusively for the private entertainment of members. The "Fourth Miscellaneous Concert" was given at the "New Theatre" again, in March, 1824, with a programme much like the last one. Rossini's "Overture to Tancred" appears "by particular request." But, evidently, the serious ambition of the Society was what were called "oratorio concerts." In April of this year it was decided to announce in the newspapers that "the Society indulge the hope that in the course of the next season, they will be enabled to present to the public some of the works of the im-

MUSICAL FUND SOCIETY

mortal Händel, both sacred and secular, by the performance of The Grand Dettingen Te Deum, and the Serenata of Acis and Galatea. . . ."

One of the above-mentioned offers came from the vestry of St. Andrew's Church, of the use of the church for oratorio in consideration of the right to hold certain rehearsals of the church chorus in the practising hall (Carpenters') of the Society. The Society allowed the latter without claiming the former.

Another proposition seems to have come from none other than the University of Pennsylvania. At a meeting in April the Building Committee was directed to confer with a committee of the trustees of the University "upon the subject of a building, proposed to be erected, with authority to devise a plan for uniting the efforts of both institutions for that purpose." From a later report it appears that the trustees finally declined to co-operate with the Society in building a hall.

The next refuge during the homeless period was St. Stephen's Church, in which the third performance of "The Creation" was given by the Society in April, 1824.

The advertisement reads strangely to our conception of early church traditions.

"The orchestra," it was promised, "will be as complete as at the performance in the Washington Hall in 1822, and, to prevent inconvenience from the church being crowded, the number of tickets for sale will be limited."

A sign of the ambitious attitude of the Society in the early years is the appointment of a "committee to inquire into the expediency of contributing a fund for the distribution of premiums for original compositions by members of the Society."

MUSICAL FUND SOCIETY

CHAPTER VI. BUILDING OF THE HALL.

THE great undertaking was definitely set in motion at a meeting in April, 1824. A loan of $10,000 was authorized; details were provided for payment of interest and principal from the perfected income. The committee were permitted to pledge the hall and lot by mortgage. Next month it was resolved to recommend to the Committee on Finance to invest in the loan the amount of the permanent fund and a part of the contingent. The lot which was in view and finally bought was that occupied by the corporation known as the Fifth Presbyterian Church. Theirs was a queer-shaped building, with a circular front on Locust Street. From its appearance it was often called the D meeting-house. Between the building and the street was a green sward, with some dozen tombstones. On the west side, at the corner of Blackberry Alley, was a two-story parsonage, which was not destroyed with the church building. The surroundings, it seems, were considered objectionable by the members. On the site was built the Musical Fund Hall.

On May 15, 1824, the building committee presented a plan for the hall, which was approved. The credit of designing a concert hall which is not surpassed for acoustic excellence, belongs to William Strickland. One of the original members of the Society, he was from the beginning undoubtedly the controlling counsellor in the matter of building. The Society had at the outset the good fortune of enrolling prominent professional men on its list. One of the most distinguished of these was the painter Thomas Sully, who was regularly called upon to make the portraits of those who had deserved well of the Society. To have an inscribed monument in St. Peter's church-yard, and one's portrait painted by Thomas Sully, were the highest honors within the dreams of a member. Physicians are perhaps most prominent of all professions. The early presidents were doctors. Lawyers are not far behind in capturing the offices. The first two secretaries were members of the bar. Names well known in finance appear early on the list of members. Indeed, the roll of names throughout the period of the Society's brilliant activity seems to represent very fairly

MUSICAL FUND SOCIETY

the best citizens, in their various lines, a true aristocracy, not a conventional. The even distribution of names among the several professions is no weak test of the homogeneous quality of musical taste and culture. It is very doubtful if to-day the love of music is equally wide-spread. There could have been in those days none of the pride in musical ignorance which it is common to see boasted. On the other hand, musical cliques were probably less marked.

With a strange absence of flourish and festivity the first concert in the new hall was given on December 29, 1824. But the high worth of the programme seems all the greater. On the line of composers' names Händel stands four times, Mozart twice. The long-promised "Dettingen Te Deum" filled all of Part I. A little book comes down to us which may have been in lieu of a programme or in supplement. It is clad in the plainest of stout blue paper. But the type is clear, strong, well varied, and perfect. We should like to give more than the title-page.

The
WORDS
of the
DETTINGEN TE DEUM
of
HAENDEL

MUSIC IN PHILADELPHIA

and of a
Miscellaneous Act
of
Vocal and Instrumental Music
as performed by the

MUSICAL FUND SOCIETY
of
Philadelphia
At the Opening of their new Hall, December 29th, 1824.
With Notes
Critical and Explanatory, &c.

Philadelphia
Published for the Musical Fund Society
by T. DeSilver.
1824.

We are sure there can be nothing new. What we think the very latest fashion in programmes is here anticipated to the last dot of detail. With the words are appended finely analytic comments, written with learning and imagination, covering every phrase of the music, just as they appear on the most modern of concert books. The whole is composed in the most serious vein, but with great simplicity. The only allusion to the occasion of the opening of the hall is concealed towards the end of an account of the Te Deum: "The Board of Directors of the Music, delegated by the Musical Fund Society, to arrange their pub-

MUSICAL FUND SOCIETY

lic concerts, conceived that they could not make a better selection for a public performance of a Society, ostensibly formed to improve the public taste in the higher branches of this art, than by the choice of a work that has stood the test of nearly a century of years. . . . At the same time the chaunting forth of praises to the Great Supreme, in strains as exalted as these, naturally leads the mind to contemplate that providence which has aided an infant society, formed for the laudable purpose of cultivating a delightful art, and of extending benevolence to our fellow-creature, so far as to enable it to struggle through its first difficulties and eventually to raise a noble structure, alike ornamental and honorable to this city. It may then, in a humble sense, be considered as a consecration anthem for the most capacious saloon in the American continent, and the first and only one devoted to musical science." . . .

Various impressions come from further reading. Händel must have been sung and studied in the city to an extent that would probably be surprising. But the landmarks of musical criticism and estimate are amusing, even startling. For example, in a voluminous subnote, we are told that "Purcell is as much the boast of England in

MUSIC IN PHILADELPHIA

music as Shakespeare in the drama." ...
Most interesting to thinkers on musical
history must be the note on the "period
that the modern school of composition
began. It has been generally dated from
Händel; by some from Purcell; as they,
certainly, more than their predecessors,
added the charms of melody to the beauty
of harmony; some, for the same reason,
go as far back as Ralestria (Palæstrina?)
... or Carissimi. ... Others with more
propriety date at the period immediately
subsequent to Händel; and undoubtedly
Bach and Abel, in their overtures, Boccherini in his Quartetts and Quintetts (1766),
Gallupi in his operas (1746) and Clementi
in his 'Piano-Forte Sonatas' (1772) changed
the style. ... Perhaps it might not be
wide of the mark to date from 1500 ... to
1700, for the old school; from then to 1800,
the middle school; from then to the present
time (embracing the labors of Beethoven,
Reis, Cherubini, Romberg, etc.) as the
modern school, leaving the three great
names of Händel, Haydn, and Mozart as
the splendid luminaries of their respective
periods." What a jumble of perspective
in an equal linking of Bach and Abel, and
of poor Beethoven with Reis and Romberg.
It is clear, too, that Beethoven was not

MUSICAL FUND SOCIETY

thought of in the same plane with Mozart; perhaps because he was almost a contemporary. They are probably misappreciated in the same ratio as were later Mendelssohn and Schumann. There are some newspaper comments on the concert.

"On Wednesday evening the grand saloon in the elegant building erected by the Musical Fund Society in Locust Street was opened for the Society's first concert this season, which was graced by the appearance of a crowded and brilliant audience of about five hundred gentlemen and eight hundred ladies, including a great portion of the fashion, beauty, and taste of our city.

"The room is exceedingly neat, and its decoration does honor to the taste of Mr. Strickland, an architect of whom Philadelphia may be justly proud. It is truly *simplex munditiis*. It is one hundred and six feet long, sixty wide, and twenty-six high, and is admirably calculated for the conveyance of sound. . . . Gentlemen who have visited most parts of Europe declare they have never been in a room superior in this respect, and in few equals. The orchestra (balcony) at the north end is judiciously arranged, so as to afford a satisfactory view of the performers to the auditors at the other extremity.

". . . The second Act was a mélange, better suited to the general taste than the first, as it consisted of a rich variety of selections, made with great skill and judgment.

". . . The band (chorus?) was very powerful, consisting of about eighty gentlemen and twenty ladies, amateurs."

MUSIC IN PHILADELPHIA

From the first report of the Building Committee it appears that the corner-stone was laid on May 25, 1824; on the 4th of November of the same year the first practising was held in the lower rooms. The building was completely finished on December 24. Of Strickland, the architect, the committee say that he executed his "important trust with the greatest faithfulness and ability."

The actual cost of the building

was	$12,968.56,
of the lot	7,500.00,
of the furniture	2,219.51,
of incidentals	859.01,
making the total	$23,547.08.

This amount was covered in approximately equal portions by a loan, for which shares were issued, and by a mortgage. From the beginning the rooms were rented successfully. Before long the income from this source alone was no inconsiderable proportion of the original outlay. In this first report the committee could say that, as the rent covered the annual interest, the Society had the use of the building free of cost. Before its completion the Masonic Hall and Washington Hall had been the principal places for concerts and balls; but the new and beautiful saloon of the Musical Fund

MUSICAL FUND SOCIETY

Hall, with its wonderful acoustic quality, soon made it the most popular place for the best kind of all entertainments. Built to satisfy the needs of the Society, it undoubtedly reacted on the musical life of the community by attracting all the famous virtuosi of the time. University and college commencements were regularly held there. Now to the reader of its programmes pass in sight, as in a camera obscura, the principal figures in the public view,—besides musicians, many of the leading orators and statesmen.

MUSIC IN PHILADELPHIA

CHAPTER VII. EARLY PLANS AND EXPERIMENTS OF THE SOCIETY.

NOTHING was stipulated in the constitution or by-laws of the Society in regard to the number of concerts to be given or about their nature. The double aim of financial relief and the improvement of musical taste was stated in analogy with the two classes of professional and amateur members; and the Committee on Music, or the Directors of the Music were "especially charged with the suggestion of such measures" as might promote the latter object. The average number of concerts during the early period was two a year. Sometimes there were more; sometimes none.

A very important adjunct from the beginning was the orchestra, which was always efficient in the quality, if not in the number of its force. Largely professional, there seems to have been no bar to the co-operation of amateur members. None of its institutions was more essential to the musical independence and influence of

EIGHTH CONCERT

OF THE

MUSICAL FUND SOCIETY

OF

PHILADELPHIA.

TO TAKE PLACE IN THEIR HALL

ON

TUESDAY, MARCH 22, 1825.

PLAN OF THE CONCERT.

PART I.

OVERTURE, De la féte du village voisin. - - - - - *Boiéldieu*
DUETT.   REST HOLY PILGRIM.   *E. Phelps*
    Rest holy pilgrim! rest I pray,
    Dreary, to Mecca's shrine's the way.   *Miss Taws*
    O! deign a Hermit's hut to share,   *and*
    Nor proudly spurn his homely fare.   *Mr. Cross.*

MUSICAL FUND SOCIETY

the Society. This was felt by the directors and by the prominent professional members. Unfortunately the *furor* for famous singers, chiefly of the Italian school, spoiled the general appreciation for the great instrumental works of the German masters. From the beginning, too, there was a chorus consisting mostly of amateur members. This was an expression, in more than one sense, of that healthy desire for the great oratorios of Händel and Haydn. The first triumphs of the Society were earned and oft repeated in performances of the "Creation." Later the "Messiah" and the "Seasons" were given. From a critical stand-point, perhaps, the soundest taste in the community prevailed in the first quarter of the century, although there was least pretence or consciousness of being in the fashion. There is a queer old leaf from the "eighth concert," of Tuesday, March 22, 1825, in fine, substantial old type, where the names of the singers had to be supplied in ink. Chief of these was Elizabeth Jefferson Fisher, the Miss Jefferson of the famous actor family, an aunt of our own Rip Van Winkle. The concert was one of the last before the Italian period. First comes an overture by Boieldieu; later another by Mehul; a third by Paer; the last two, examples of the purest of that sober age. Interspersed are such perennial songs as Bishop's "Bid me Discourse." Not since then have singers had the courage to bring the English song-classics back to the concert stage.

Largely with a view to the improvement of the orchestra, partly, perhaps, in a spirit of ambitious venture, a committee reported, in May, 1825, in favor of establishing a school of music, which, "owing to the progressive decay of our orchestra, has become almost necessary to our existence." It was intended largely as a feeder of instrumental material. The plan was rapidly set in motion. In December the "Committee on the Academy of Music" made a final report, saying that it had begun on the 12th of September with two departments,—one for violins, 'cellos, and bass, the other for wind instruments. Teachers were engaged at regular salaries. In the mean time, in June, had been given the ninth concert, very much like the one last described. The tenth was "The Creation," and the eleventh a fine blending of Paer, Haydn, Beethoven, and Boccherini, with some good songs. Of this kind of evening there were too many to mention.

MUSICAL FUND SOCIETY

These were really the good old times for musical taste. One concert in particular was given on July 19, 1825, in aid of some "Hospitable Society." There is a Gluck overture and seven Händel numbers: airs and choruses.

Miss Jefferson sang again; it was the time of Lafayette's second visit. The managers of the Society requested a committee to invite him to attend the concert. Lafayette wrote in answer:

"NEW YORK, July 6th, 1825.

"I do not think it will be in my power to reach Philadelphia before the end of next week. The concert might then take place on some early day of the week following. I anticipate much pleasure the moment I can offer you in person the affectionate regard of your sincere friend.

"LAFAYETTE."

All of this was printed, with the programme, as an announcement of the concert. The details of Lafayette's visit are known. He attended the concert, and, we are told, attracted much attention.

In the spirit of the "Academy" other plans were considered. In 1826 the trustees of the latter recommended the establishment of a vocal class.

A resolution passed "that a musical journal, to be published in quarterly numbers of about 100 pages each, be established under the patronage of this Society, provided that a reasonable assurance can be obtained that its publication will not infringe on the funds of the Society." The next step was a proposition to the Academy of Fine Arts to join in the enterprise. The title was to be

THE AMERICAN JOURNAL
of the
FINE ARTS

Conducted by a Joint Committee
of the
Pennsylvania Academy of Fine Arts
and the
Musical Fund Society of Philadelphia.

The subjects of which the journal shall consist shall be Music, Poetry, Painting, Sculpture, Engraving, and Architecture. The journal to be conducted by a joint committee of six members, etc. etc.

The directors of the "Academy" agreed to the plan. Committees were appointed; all formal steps were taken. For some reason this idea, so beautiful in conception, was never realized. Perhaps it was smothered in the pomp of preparatory detail.

The orchestra and the chorus were permanent institutions. On every programme

MUSICAL FUND SOCIETY

there was an imposing array of *conductors*, for example:

Instrumental. — Messrs. Hommann, Sr., Hupfeld, and Le Roy.

Vocal.—Messrs. B. Carr, Cross, and T. Loud.

Leader.—Mr. Hupfeld.

In the high hopes for the fruits of the "Academy," the Society engaged Adolph Schmitz, a Düsseldorf musician, to come to Philadelphia and take charge of the third class in the "Academy." Mr. Schmitz became a distinguished teacher in the city. Here is a single instance where the Society was the cause of a great musical gain to the city, directly in the elder Schmitz, indirectly in the younger, who soon became foremost among the local musicians.

Outside of the regular and special concerts given under the management of the directors were, of course, a long line of virtuosi who rented the hall on their own enterprise. One of the first, in more than the sense of time, of the brilliant Italian singers who trod the boards of our hall in their triumphal processions, was Madame Malibran, who sang on June 16, 1827, under the name of Signorina. In the newspapers the announcement was of

MUSIC IN PHILADELPHIA

SIGNORINA'S CONCERT.

The programme was surprisingly good. Of instrumental numbers three were by Haydn, one by Mozart. Signorina sang Gluck's "Che faro;" Mozart's "Batti batti;" and Rossini's "Di tanti palpiti," and some other songs. Malibran was so much pleased with the acoustic virtues of the saloon that, when the concert was over, she walked up and down extemporizing, while Da Coninck, who "presided at the piano," played an accompaniment.

At the second of the "Signorina" concerts, however, seven of the ten numbers were from Rossini.

The Garcia Opera Troupe, under the management of Manuel Garcia, father of Madame Malibran, was the first to introduce Italian opera in the United States. The experiment was considered problematical, and, in fact, the opera failed as a financial venture. But the personal triumph of Malibran was unquestioned, and, in striking exception, it preceded her successful *début* in Europe. The essence of her power, so far as we may gather at second hand, must have lain in the sensitiveness of a temperament which would prompt her on the stage to the most daring feats of improvisation in cadences. It was in a memorable contest

MUSICAL FUND SOCIETY

with Caradori Allen, in Manchester, England, that a supreme effort was thought by some to have caused her death, which followed soon after. At any rate it was her swan song. To complete our picture of this concert in its reality, we must import a prosaic element from the notice in Poulson's "Daily Advertiser:" "Nearly all the seats in the lower tier and a great part of the second tier of boxes were occupied by ladies in full dress, which gave great brilliancy to the house, however badly supported by the gloomy and dreary light. It is much to be desired that our enterprising manager . . . will, in the future, remedy that evil, by substituting gas-light . . . or add a large middle chandelier to the present order." Gas was not introduced in the hall, however, until ten years later, in September, 1837.

The old concerts still went on. The great event of 1828 was the production of the "Messiah." The glowing reports in the "United States Gazette" and in the "Daily Advertiser" are not reflected in the annual report of that year, where there is some grumbling about the great expense of the concert. In a programme of December of this year some of the newer romantic music has crept in: Beethoven's "Egmont" overture, and Weber's "Hunters' Chorus" from the "Freischütz." Below we had almost missed a strange old warning, which yet looks curiously new: "The concert will begin at 7 o'clock, precisely.

"To prevent an inconvenience that has formerly been complained of, it is most respectfully requested that ladies attending the concert will avoid wearing large bonnets or high head-dresses."

During the remainder of this decade the periodical concerts and the annual reports continue in much the same way. The latter are at first full of self-congratulation, later they settle down to a less fulsome self-content. Suddenly, in April, 1831, the disillusionment is faced. The committee on the "Academy" "are obliged to state that the number paying for and receiving instruction . . . amount to no more than twelve. . . . This great diminution . . . the committee cannot satisfactorily account for. They are, however, satisfied that it is not owing to an inherent defect in it, but to casual and extrinsic circumstances. It will, however, occasion a considerable expense to the Society, which, in the present state of the finances, it would have been very desirable to have avoided." Still the committee think the "Academy" ought to continue.

But a year later the discontent is more

MUSICAL FUND SOCIETY

frank and more fundamental. The whole tone is regretful. It begins with a discussion of the two controlling aims of the Society. One of the troubles seems to have been a poor attendance of the "professors" at the "practisings," which had fallen out of repute. Reproachfully the progress is recounted of public taste under the influence of the Society, and, impliedly, the increased benefit to professional musicians. "The Community of Philadelphia was not at that time (twelve years before) so critically informed of the merits of musical performances as they have since become. Public concerts had for many years been in disrepute. Instrumental pieces of whatever merit were not listened to, and the time which they occupied was generally appropriated to fashionable conversation. The private musical soirées, which are now so numerous, were rarely thought of. The primary object of the Society was to reform the state of neglect into which the beautiful art of music had fallen. That object it has effected entirely and beyond a question. Nothing can be more unlike than the present conduct and opinions of the people of Philadelphia in all that relates to music and their conduct and opinions twelve years ago." Here it is shown how the second object, the provision of a relief fund, has been fulfilled. "Yet," they frankly continue, "the Society is on the decline," speaking from a purely financial stand-point. Finally, they object "to appropriating any longer $700 *per annum* to keep up the school with the expense exceeding the receipts by the amount." In July, action was taken in accordance with this report. Thus ends the "Academy." Its story pathetically shows the high ambition of the founders. Their aim was precisely right for the establishment of the best kind of performances by the perfection of a local orchestra. But this part of the Society's work was least supported by the public. Besides, the idea of an annexed school for the exclusive purpose of developing an orchestra involved means quite out of proportion to the aim. Still the aim must always be higher than the gain.

Together with this change, others were soon adopted. The most important were the reduction of the musical session from eight to six months; abolishing of the practisings; in lieu of the former sixteen practisings, an additional public concert and three private "soirées" were provided.

The first great loss of the Society happened in May, 1831, in the death of Benjamin Carr. The tributes paid him have been described in an earlier chapter.

MUSICAL FUND SOCIETY

CHAPTER VIII. FIGURES OF THE TIME.

E come now to the period 1830–40. Musically it is not specially important. I propose, therefore, that we transform ourselves into some insect—a spider, say—harbored in a corner of the hall, with a good view of the stage, and out of danger from the janitor. Without admission ticket, with a sort of stolen life-membership, we can then watch all the figures as they come and go; on the platform, in the strain and dignity of their tasks; on the floor, in unconscious bustle and irresponsible enjoyment. We can see the whole scene, too, gradually brighten from flickering oil to—well a very wonderful new invention in lighting, however ill constituted to cast reflections on its predecessor.

First of all, what a magnificent array of American statesmen throng the hall day after day of a week in the early autumn of 1831; some of them of permanent fame, all representative of foremost citizenship.

MUSIC IN PHILADELPHIA

There was "a convention of the advocates of free trade, without distinction of party, . . . two hundred and twelve delegates. Among them were Theodore Sedgwick, George Peabody, and John L. Gardner, from Massachusetts; Preserved Fish, John Constable, John A. Stevens, Jonathan Goodhue, . . . and Albert Gallatin, from New York; C. C. Biddle, George Emlen, Isaac W. Norris, from Pennsylvania; Jos. W. Allston and Wm. C. Preston, from South Carolina, and men of equal distinction, bankers, merchants, statesmen, and political economists from other States. Of this convention, Gallatin was the soul. Mr. Gallatin found himself in direct opposition to Mr. Clay, whose political existence was staked upon the opposite theory. Mr. Clay answered in a great speech in the Senate, in February, 1832, personally denouncing Mr. Gallatin as a foreigner with European interests at heart. For this he expressed his regret to Mr. Gallatin in an interview arranged by mutual friends at a much later period."* Chief Justice Marshall was present at the meeting on the fourth day. Here is a momentous council within these our modest walls. And, in

---

* Life of Gallatin, by Stevens.

MUSICAL FUND SOCIETY

truth, we do hear some ungracious objections to the hall, and much grumbling that the city had no other provision. Otherwise, the talk, I dare say, sounds much like some very familiar arguments that are still beaten back and forth.

Next is a "meeting of the friends of the Constitution and of Domestic Industry, . . . on Thursday, January 24th, 1832, in relation to the alarming and momentous crisis in the affairs of the country, menacing the integrity of the Union by the assertion of the Nullification Acts on the part of the State of South Carolina." The Mayor presides, but there do not seem to be any eminent figures. It is an early symptom of a national disease, wellnigh fatal, now happily and entirely cured.

On the last day of this year we have a pageant of the famous old bar of Philadelphia. The Hon. John Sergeant delivers a eulogy on the life and character of Charles Carroll, of Carrollton, and is listened to by the Judges of the Courts, members of Congress and of the Legislature, Provost and Faculty of the University, the Reverend Clergy, the Mayor, Aldermen, High Sheriff, of the city, etc., etc.

But, speaking of pageants, what must we expect from the promises of this notice:

MUSIC IN PHILADELPHIA

ANNUAL COMMENCEMENT
of the

UNIVERSITY OF PENNSYLVANIA

July 25, 1833

A procession will be formed and will move from the College Hall Ninth Street at 10 A. M. in the following order

Janitor of the College
Students of the Collegiate Department
Faculty of Arts
Provost
President of the Board of Trustees
Trustees of the University
Candidates for the Degree of A. B.
Candidates for the Degree of A. M.
Janitor of the Medical Department
Faculty of Medicine
Professors of Other Colleges
Alumni of the University
Honorary Members of the Philomathean and
Zelosophic Societies
Students in the Medical Schools
Professors in the Medical Schools
Instructors in the University
Principals and Teachers in the Academical
Department
Teachers in the University Charity Schools
Teachers of Philadelphia
Reverend Clergy
Judges of the Court of the United States
United States Senators
Members of the House of Representatives of the
United States

MUSICAL FUND SOCIETY

Judges of the Supreme Court of Pennsylvania
Judges of the District Court
Judges of the Court of Common Pleas
Speaker of the Senate of Pennsylvania
State Senators
Members of the House of Representatives
Mayor of the City
Recorder and Aldermen
Members of the Select and Common Councils
Justices of the Peace
Strangers invited to attend the Commencement
Citizens

The procession will move through Ninth to Chestnut, through Chestnut to Eighth, through Eighth to Locust, through Locust to the Hall of the Musical Fund Society.

Here we are in a strongly academic atmosphere, which is, however, still fragrant to-day, though more faintly. But how the janitors have fallen from their high estate! Another political meeting early in the next year on a red-hot national question, which has not entirely cooled down today, "of citizens opposed to the removal of the Government deposits from the United States Bank and the many usurpations of Andrew Jackson, and who are desirous of transmitting to their descendants, in all its original purity, the Constitution they have received from their sires." The meeting was held at half-past three o'clock. The

MUSIC IN PHILADELPHIA

hall was filled and many had to stay outside.

Once more let the lawyers take the floor: A fitting occasion for a parade of a noted bar; an inspiring theme, though grave; an orator who will rise to its full dignity. In September, 1835, Horace Binney delivers a eulogy on Chief Justice Marshall, which is again attended by the formidable line of Mayor, Aldermen, Judges, etc., etc. Among the clergy is Bishop White, in his clerical robes. They meet at Independence Hall and march in procession to Musical Fund. Two-thirds of the audience are ladies. There are present Bishops Moore, of Virginia; Doane, of New Jersey; Onderdonk, of New York; Smith, of Kentucky; Onderdonk, of Pennsylvania, and some others. Bishop White opens the meeting with prayer. The address, we are assured, is "not merely a eulogy," but "an instructive lesson upon the past." It occupies an hour and three-quarters in the delivery. Many have to stand; others are unable to gain admittance.

It seems to have been a habit of those days to hold public memorial meetings over deceased men of eminence. The tendency since then has been to draw back in our expression of condolence within the privacy

MUSICAL FUND SOCIETY

of the profession. It is probable that the press has made these public meetings obsolete by its prompt obituaries and editorials, which leave little to be said a few days later. In the quickness of modern life, every event is followed by immediate comment and passes away. The real meeting of condolence consists now of telegraphed messages and of oral expressions reported in the hour of their first utterance. They certainly have the great merit, besides informality, of spontaneity. Musical Fund Hall probably saw a solemn succession of these funereal orations, chiefly of the members of the bar,—who could supply subject and orator of high eminence. On December 31st, 1836, a eulogy is held, by David Paul Brown, on the eminent lawyer, William Rawle.

But, in general, it must have been the time when the idea of the popular lecture first occurred to the enthusiastic minds of people who know a little. It must have been a special want, and a special boon to cities in proportion to their distance from the centres of thought, and in a much greater ratio than to-day. So we find in the "United States Gazette" of the 7th of December, 1837, a notice that the Athenian Institute had been "lately formed with the view of procuring the delivery of public lectures on popular subjects during the winter season." Party politics and sectarian religion were alone excepted. Officers were prominent physicians and lawyers. So long ago it is noteworthy that physicians took the intellectual lead in Philadelphia,— indeed, in music, much more than to-day. There is a long list of "Counsellors,"— twenty-five; not a few are still famous. The idea was undoubtedly to supply voluntary lectures from their own number. There is nothing provincial about a course of lectures by men like the Sergeants, Ingersolls, and Rawles of the bar, like Rev. W. H. Furness or Professor Henry Reed. Strange to say, there was much competition between rival societies. The Mercantile Library Association advertised its first course to begin in November, 1839. The lecturers who had promised were men of similar distinction. There were Wm. M. Meredith and Geo. M. Dallas. Some of the "Counsellors" of the Institute appear on the list. Indeed, the latter organization seems to have been crowded out by the later one. Both used the Musical Fund Hall. Besides local volunteers, as we suppose they were, this new fashion of lectures brings before us various public figures, much as they

MUSICAL FUND SOCIETY

still appear to-day. But then the emphasis was upon the lecture, not upon the mere sight of a "celebrity." The attraction lay in the merits of the address; lecturing was itself more of a profession. They pass along in motley line: John B. Gough, the reclaimed drunkard; Edward Everett, the New England statesman; Samuel Lover, Irish novelist; Horace Mann, on "Great Britain." Tremendous titles: Joseph R. Chandler, on the "Dignity of Man;" Professor Silliman, on a scientific subject much too long to repeat; Caleb Cushing has his day, on "India," and R. H. Dana, Jr., on "American Loyalty." In 1842 comes George Bancroft, who was even then an authority on "The American Revolution;" after him, in almost successive weeks, Ralph Waldo Emerson, William H. Furness, and Horace Greeley. A brilliant course for the Friday evenings of the Mercantile Library. But the Athenians still held to their regular Tuesdays, with local prophets.

A complete list of lectures in so representative a hall must be a fair index of the history of the intellectual life of the community. However, that is not the present purpose. But here are a few suggestive titles. "Yankee" Hill on "The Manners and Customs of the People of New England" must have been one of the humorists of the day. So was "Mr. Roberts, comedian," who "will be at home . . . and deliver a lecture (in three parts) on the character, peculiarities, and manners of John Bull," etc., etc., with an enumeration of detail like the advertisement of a country circus. Here is one we can easily guess the temper of: "Dickens, or the English tourist in America," a lecture delivered in March, 1843.

Add to this the list of "Commencements" of all kinds, exhibitions of musical "seminaries," the great balls of the season, and, above all, the great occasions to which the building was dedicated, and you have perhaps as complete a history of the people as you might gather a few blocks away from official archives.

MUSICAL FUND SOCIETY

CHAPTER IX. ENGLISH MUSICIANS IN PHILADELPHIA.

IN the splendor of the Italians, whose names, at least, are always high-sounding, we are apt to forget the plain-titled English musicians. Their influence, always for good, was subtle in its working. They lacked the prestige and dash of the Italian. Philadelphia was specially helped by their coming. Indeed, there seemed to be a peculiar mutual attraction between the Quakers and that type of thorough, conscientious musician, high-toned in the best sense. From the earliest times we have traced, until the present, he has singled out the city of the Friends, and it has always responded with respect, if not with fervor. The men who first stirred musical desire and urged organized enterprise were now departing. Almost simultaneously with the death of Carr came that of Schetky, of whom we have spoken above. A concert for the benefit of his family was given in December, 1831. There was left the youngest of the trio, Benjamin

MUSIC IN PHILADELPHIA

Cross, who maintained the early traditions of his teachers, transmitting them to a younger member of his own family, in whom the city may well take pride, as one of its leading musicians. The loss of Carr and Schetky was in some degree mended by the arrival of another Englishman, Charles Jarvis, an excellent pianist and, secondarily, a composer. Again, in his case, the greatest service lay in the permanent devotion of his life to high musical standards. He was thus, in turn, the cause of the acquisition, in his son Charles J. Jarvis, of a pianist than whom America has never produced an equal in the combination of certain high qualities: of broad scholarship, of profound critical power, of a wonderful degree of technique as performer, of absolutely disinterested pursuit of the highest standard in the building of his programmes. The quality and power of his calibre were very like those of the late Hans von Bulow; but fortune cast him on different soil. It is clear that from the beginning the city was fortunate in the residence of men, mostly English, who joined to their intellectual breadth the moral power to resist the temptation of artistic demagogism.

Aside from the men who came to stay, this particular period of the second quarter

MUSICAL FUND SOCIETY

of the century is very full of English musical visitors. They are more especially in danger of oblivion because of the triumphant march, upon their heels, of the famous band of singers and players from Southern Europe. With the latter the stress was all in the quality of performance, in the turn of the note; they introduced to Americans the wonders of the virtuoso *par éminence*. The English, on the other hand, with less heralding, had more substantial wares. They were often far more than singers. In introducing their own compositions they had an influence which, though less immediate, was more far-reaching. A record of their work is as deserved as it is interesting.

There is always some queen of song, some *diva*, who commands the superlatives, however short be her reign. They are as frequent, as tyrannous, and as ephemeral as popular songs. Each in her turn is unsurpassed,—until her successor appears. It means, of course, nothing else than the power of the personal woman. The voice is really of no importance other than as a medium for carrying the personal message. The audience is like the fickle lover who is sincere enough for a time. There can of course be nothing but superlatives. There

MUSIC IN PHILADELPHIA

must be unconditional conquest or there is a failure. We might moralize. Either it is all a mere play, a self-deception, or, more likely, a temporary state of emotional excitement which takes no account of other conditions and relations,—where judgment takes a holiday. There is perhaps little to choose between the two solutions. But it is a kind of deduction to say that the more the personality of the performer beclouds the actual music, the further is the result from the fine end and purpose of the art.

In our survey of English visitors, there are three kinds: one came originally and directly to stay and teach; others passed through on their planetic orbit; but there were some who came with this same triumphant impulse, but somehow lost momentum. Often they were too old for the genuine ring. Perhaps they honestly changed their minds, preferring to stay.

But it was a common phrase, that America was the burying-ground of English artists.

One of these was Charles Edward Horn, an English singer and composer. He had been successful at the Drury Lane and the Lyceum Theatres. On his several visits he became familiar to Philadelphians. Finally he settled in Boston, first as conductor of

MUSICAL FUND SOCIETY

the Händel and Haydn Society. Towards the last he kept a music store.

The queen at this particular time, the third decade of the century, was undoubtedly the famous Mrs. Austin. We are convinced of this, not so much by the size of the type on the programmes, or by the noise of praise, as by an unconscious implication in an estimate of a rival. There was a Madame Feron, an Englishwoman better known as Mrs. Glossop. An English critic of the time called her second to no Italian but Pasta. A later annalist, after praising her voice and method, adds that some preferred her to Mrs. Austin.* Both singers appeared at the Musical Fund Hall. Madame Feron sang Italian arias, — one " composed expressly for her by Donizetti." Mrs. Austin sang English and Italian songs in November, 1833. There is a queer old programme which has fluttered down to us, with enormous names on a short leaf. Somehow we are less attracted by the famous lady than by the announcement of a Mr. Power, who "has in the kindest manner volunteered Two Irish Melodies." He looks like a noble pioneer of a worthy line of Briton singers, of whom

---

* Richard Grant White, in the "Century Magazine."

MUSIC IN PHILADELPHIA

the last, also an Irishman, seems strangely like this early kinsman. By one account Tyrone Power was born in 1795, the son of an Irish gentleman of the County of Waterford. "He afterwards became famous in Irish comedy and as a singer of Irish songs." We are told that he wrote well; that he published some impressions of America in 1836, besides two novels.* We believe this praise. There are some verses which he wrote on board the "Algonquin," which we had almost published in full. It is a simple song of farewell, with true feeling.

"I've pierced from North to South thy eternal woods,
  Have dream'd in fair St. Lawrence's sweetest isle,
  Have breasted Mississippi's hundred floods,
  And wooed on Allegheny's top Aurora's smile."

Then a verse homeward sung. But once more he turns with generous words:

"Welcome and home were mine within the land,
  Whose sons I leave, whose fading shore I see;
  And cold must be my eyes, and heart and hand,
  When, fair Columbia! they turn cold to thee."

Power sailed for the last time for England on the steamship "President," in March,

---
* See Allibone's Musical Dictionary.

MUSICAL FUND SOCIETY

1841. Some may still remember the widespread sensation that the total loss of the vessel and of her passengers caused. Here is part of a lament of Washington Irving's:

"What sighs have been wafted after that ship! What prayers offered up at the deserted fireside of home! How often has the mistress, the wife, the mother, pored over the daily papers, to catch some casual intelligence of the victims of the deep! How has expectation darkened into anxiety, anxiety into dread, and dread into despair! Alas! not one memento shall ever return for love to cherish! All that shall ever be known is that she sailed from her port, and was never heard of more!"

In 1834 the great favorites in concert and opera were Mr. and Mrs. Wood, as they were very simply announced. The lady had succeeded in London as Miss Paton, had married a Lord Lenox who ill-treated her. Divorced from him, she accepted one Joseph Wood, a pugilist, with an untrained voice. Strangely enough, it was by introducing the delights of Italian opera that the Woods won their great American fame, chiefly in an English version of "La Sonnambula," which carried everything by storm. Even now old people will roll their eyes in memory of those delights. "'Still so gently o'er me stealing' or 'Hear me swear now' were heard from the throats of singers, the fingers of piano-forte thrummers, and even the lips of whistlers. . . . Mrs. Wood was worshipped as if she had been a beauty."* Later, in 1840, the Woods appeared at the Chestnut Street Theatre in a version of "Norma." The whole performance was memorable, with an orchestra of fifty and a chorus of one hundred, drilled by Wm. H. Fry, a well-known composer and critic, and composed of members of the various singing societies and choirs of the cities. "Ladies and gentlemen," it is recorded, "of distinguished talents in the musical circles of the city did not hesitate to take part. The theatre was crowded for twenty consecutive nights, and the occasion was long remembered as that of a brilliant operatic triumph." It was the first production of "Norma" in this country. But here comes a yellow page from a regular Society concert in 1834, in which Mr. and Mrs. Wood are announced. There is nowhere a suggestion of Italian enchantment. The orchestra played Beethoven's "Egmont" overture, and the Woods sang each a grand

---

* R. G. White in the "Century."

MUSICAL FUND SOCIETY

scene from "Der Freischütz," besides some plain English ballads.

Midst the intoxication over "Sonnambula" and "Norma," there must have been a very serious time for those good people—and there were many in those days—whose long-rooted principles forbade gazing at a regular grand opera. So we have a pathetic notice: In May, 1836, "to meet the wishes of numerous parties who do not visit the theatres," Mr. and Mrs. Wood "will give selections from 'La Sonnambula,' with full band accompaniments and numerous choruses."

A number of singers appear so often in such very large type that they must have been very remarkable. They have all indubitably English names. There were Mrs. and Miss Watson; Mrs. Wheatly; Mr. and Mrs. Morely; Mrs. Gibbs; James Howard, a very sweet-toned tenor. They were of the band who introduced the book of English songs old and new, which have since become household classics all over the land.

There is one Englishman who deserves a full share of attention, partly for the songs he wrote and sang, more still for the unconscious humor of his announcements. Henry Russell was a singer who evidently

MUSIC IN PHILADELPHIA

confined himself to his own songs. Here is a typical programme.

MR. H. RUSSELL

will give a grand concert at the Musical Fund Hall on Saturday evening, May 15th (1841), on which occasion Mr. Russell will introduce several of his latest compositions which have met with so much applause in Boston and New York.

PART I.

Song "I love, I love the free"   Russell
    "The wild stream leaps with headlong sweep."

Song "In the days when we went gipsying a long time ago"   arranged by Russell

Song "The old Sexton" [Words by Park Benjamin]

"Nigh to a grave that was newly made
Leaned a sexton old, on his earth-worn spade;
His work was done, and he paused to wait,
The funeral train through the open gate;
A relic of bygone days was he,
And his locks were white as the foaming sea;
And these words came from his lips so thin,
I gather them in! I gather them in!"

Song "Wind of the winter's night, whence comest thou?" A descriptive poem by Charles Mackay   Russell

Song "The Ivy Green." Words by Boz   Russell

Song "Arm, brothers, arm! I've lost my child! The wolf is out!"
[A description of a wolf-hunt]   Russell

MUSICAL FUND SOCIETY

New Song "We were boys together"   Russell
   [The words written by G. P. Morris.]
Song "The Maniac." [Words partly by Monk
      Lewis.]   Russell

The above description of a scene in a Mad House is founded on fact. Some years since a gentleman of large fortune was taken to a Mad House and there confined seven feet under ground. The persons that accompanied him took oath, to those entrusted with the care of the establishment, to the fact of his being a maniac. The more the poor fellow implored for his release, the more forcibly was the keeper convinced. The treatment he received while thus confined affected his reason, and he became frantic and shortly died from the effect. The strangers that carried him to the Mad House were supposed to have been hired by some brutal relatives, who at his death were to come in possession of his property.

PART II.

Song "Come, brothers, arouse, arouse!"   Russell

Song Descriptive—"The Gambler's Wife"   Russell
   Words written expressly for Mr. Russell by
      Dr. Coates, by particular request.

"Dark is the night! How dark! No light! No fire!
Cold on the hearth the last faint sparks expire!
Shivering she watches by the cradle side,
For him who pledged her love! Last year a Bride!

"Hark! 'Tis his footstep! No? 'Tis past; 'tis gone!
Tic! Tic! How wearily the time rolls on!
Why should he leave me thus? He once was kind;
And I believed 'twould last? How mad! How
    blind!

MUSIC IN PHILADELPHIA

"Rest thee, my babe! Rest on! 'Tis hunger's cry!
Sleep! For there is no food! The fount is dry!
Famine and cold their wearying work have done!
My heart must break! And thou my child—hush!
The clock strikes one!——"

This song is designed to represent the feelings of a young wife and mother, under circumstances sufficiently common to warrant the assertion that it is founded on fact, without exaggeration. It represents the gambler's wife and child, deserted by their natural protector, in the extreme of poverty and starvation, for the pleasures of play. The fire expires;—the energies of life sink for want of food, and the mother vainly strives to hope in the midst of despair, appealing to the past with the memory of the bride, while vainly endeavoring to soothe the child with the energy of a mother's love, until the infant dies in her arms and her heart is broken. The current of her feelings is interrupted only by the peal of the clock, and at the third hour the scene closes; while time strides onward, in its monotonous march, regardless, as the world, of the issue.

Song "Rockaway"

> "On Long Island's sea-girt shore
> Many an hour I've whiled away."

Words by P. H. Sharpe   Russell

Song "The Old Farm Gate"   Russell

"Where, where is that gate that used to divide
The old shaded lane from the grassy roadside?"

Song "The Old Arm Chair"   Russell

"I love it, I love it, and who shall dare
To chide me for loving that old arm chair!"

MUSICAL FUND SOCIETY

Song "Let us be gay"—a laughing chorus. Russell

Performance to commence at 8 o'clock.

Tickets 50 cents each, to be had at the principal music stores and at the door on the evening of performance.

That Russell was not taken seriously by every one is proven by a parody that appeared in a newspaper:

GRAND CONCERT

Mr. Twaddle has the honour to announce to his friends, that he will give a concert on Saturnalia evening, at the bassooneon, at seven o'clock. The music by a most eminent composer.

PART I.

Reproduction, piano forte	Tallbut
Song—"Away! away! over Back Bay, ho!"	Twaddle
Song—The Old Grist Mill	Twaddle

"Can this be the grist-mill that nine years hence
Will be taken and used for a cow-yard fence?"

Song—The Old Church Mouse   Twaddle

"Near to a pew that was newly lined
Sat an old church mouse, who had not dined," etc.

Descriptive Song—The Rowdy—Words
written *expressly* for Mr. Twaddle. Twaddle

"Light is the room! how light—no dark—how warm!
Drunk on the floor the last young spark falls down,
Trembling, not knowing what he was about,
He babbles—' My *mother*, do you know I'm out?'

MUSIC IN PHILADELPHIA

"Hark! 'twas a cat! No 'tis a dog! No! it's Ned!
Clack! clack! Oh dear, if I *could* go ahead!
Why am I blind? I'm sure I once could see;
But eye and sight have failed. Ah, me! ah, me!

"Sleep on, old Ned! sleep on! 'Tis *nature's* cry!
The bottle's all emptied, and I am so *dry!*
Eating and drinking have made me a brute!
My poor head will split, and my brains come through!
     The bells ring for fire," etc.

[This song represents a young man under *circumstances* too common to prove an exaggeration. We see the youth deserted by his natural good sense, in the extreme of folly and drunkenness, for the *pleasures* of frolic; the fire burns bright; the muscles of his body sink from no want of stimulus; the current of his thoughts is interrupted by the entrance of a watchman; the door opens, and he struts forth with an irregular zigzag, regardless as the world of the gaze of the waiters.]

PART II.

Song—The Old Tin-Pail	Twaddle
Song—"Foot it! foot! I've lost my pig—the cow is gone!"	Twaddle
Duett—The Old Nurse-Lamp — and Old Fine-Tooth Comb	Twaddle
"Oh! deem me not an useless thing."	
Song—The Dropsical Idiot—by request.	Twaddle
Song—(new)—The Old Irish Baby	Twaddle
Song—"On Old Green Frog-Pond's rock-bound Coast"	Twaddle

MUSICAL FUND SOCIETY

The editor good-humoredly adds: "If 'he may laugh who *wins*,' Mr. Russell will relish the above as heartily as any one; for he certainly maintains his popularity with the music-loving public."

It is almost incredible that a man of solid ability could descend to such commonplace sensationalism. But there is no doubt that Russell had a vein of melody that met wide and quick acceptance. Even now one still hears songs like "A Life on the Ocean Wave;" "Cheer! Boys! Cheer!" "The Ivy Green," and others. Putting together, critically, these with many of the common college songs, one sees a clear resemblance, an undoubted descent. For instance, compare the common student song "A Home by the Sea" with "A Life on the Ocean Wave." It is quite probable that to Russell is due the vein of many songs of the college world and of summer holidays of a certain amount of vitality.

Of course, the great original of this *genre* of English composer-singers was John Braham. But he had the good sense to throw much of his power into a worthy interpretation of Händel's great arias. Born in 1774, he had practically completed his triumphant career abroad when he appeared in America. He sang in a concert at the Musical Fund

MUSIC IN PHILADELPHIA

Hall at the age of seventy. Some of his compositions remind us of the Russell kind. One was the "Village Blacksmith." Another was the "Burial of Sir Thomas Moore," which was invariably sung with a full military accompaniment of brass and drums. The latter were particularly loud during the opening line:

> "Not a drum was heard, nor a funeral note."

This proved, one day, too much for the patience of a good man in the audience, who interfered with the usual effect by calling out: "They must have been confoundedly deaf."

Probably the greatest singer of this school was one whom we have once mentioned as a rival of Malibran. Her commonest stage-name was Madame Caradori Allen. It takes a search through most of Europe to find her true nationality. It seems she was famous as Caradori before she became Mrs. Allen. Authentic information says that she was of a highly respectable German family, "daughter of Baron de Munck, a Colonel in the French army." The only high quality which, apparently, she did not possess was dramatic power. Her art was of the highest, and her influence as concert singer of the very best. She appeared

MUSICAL FUND SOCIETY

frequently at our hall on her arrival in America in 1837. Another favorite singer of Italian arias was Elizabeth Poole. One who captivated rather more by beauty of manner than of voice was Miss Jane Shireff.

Every play-goer of fifty years ago will remember Edward Seguin and his wife. They were of the many able actors and singers who visited America and found the home they had missed in England. Anne Seguin was an equal successor of the line of Mrs. Wood, Mrs. Austin, and Caradori Allen. She sang *prima donna* in most of the classical Italian operas, from *Zerlina* to *Donna Anna*. In the forties the Seguins often sang at the Walnut Street Theatre, where Benjamin C. Cross was then leader of the orchestra. Edward's voice was a deep bass. Among many *insignia* of success in America was an election as chief of an Indian tribe. Edward Kean, the tragedian, was the only other Englishman who got this honor. The Indians gave Seguin the name of "the man with the deep mellow voice."

No better sign of the vigor and direction of the work of this English tribe of singers could possibly come to light than the account of a remarkable performance of Mozart's "Magic Flute" at the Musical Fund

MUSIC IN PHILADELPHIA

Hall. The mere fact of an entire production of serious opera at the hall was, as far as the record shows, unprecedented. It was a "Grand Musical Festival" for the benefit of some "asylum"; and the public was "respectfully informed that the music of the grand opera of the 'Magic Flute,' composed by the inspired Mozart, will be performed, for the first time in America, at the Musical Fund Hall, . . . on . . . February 8th, 1841." The performers are named, down to the players of the tympani and of the bells. "Madame Otto," the notice said, "was engaged on account of the indisposition of Mrs. Seguin." The rest of the cast were: Miss Poole, Miss Thornton, Mr. Manvers, Mr. Latham, Mr. Thornton, Signor Giubilei, and Mr. Seguin. Thus, originally all but one were to be English singers. The success of the opera, in its selection, performance, and reception, is a fine gauge of public taste and of musical interest. There were sixty-four performers in the orchestra, almost all of whom were so distinguished that it was necessary to give their full names. Mr. B. C. Cross "presided at the piano," probably from force of habit. There could be no other reason in the full orchestra, which included bassethorn and ophicleide. Admission cost two

MUSICAL FUND SOCIETY

dollars. Then there was a repetition for some other "benefit." It is said that parties were made up in New York and Boston specially to enjoy the performance. Newspaper comments gave praise in the regular phrases. That of the "National Gazette" had the greatest variety of adjectives. Significant is its last paragraph : "The public has now had such samples of operatic excellence that mediocrity will no longer answer. What is now done in that way must be done fully and well to command success."

It is worth noticing that the whole enterprise was the work of a single citizen, an eminent builder of locomotives.

MUSIC IN PHILADELPHIA

CHAPTER X. SUMMUS PARNASSUS.

THE reason for tracing the career of the Musical Fund Society, especially as we approach the middle of the century, is not so much its own interest and importance, as its peculiar relation to the musical history of Philadelphia. The hall was not merely the only concert-room for Philadelphians. The dignity of the Society was, to a degree, independent of the accident of its location. Its fame and the policy of the directors brought musicians who would otherwise have passed the city by. The lustre of the Society outshone that of the city. The hall was known to the *virtuosi* of the world, who enjoyed singing or playing there for its own sake. A great musician considered a visit to the hall a necessary part of his tour. Thus, not unlike foreign cosmopolitan concert-halls, the simple minutes of the board meetings and the annual reports give a certain reflection of the musical progress of the world. Besides all this, the support of the Society, in its associate membership, had come to be representative of the city, more, perhaps, than any artistic

MUSICAL FUND SOCIETY

society then or since. Thus, for a double reason, an account of the Society in its flourishing period is a terse sketch of the attitude of Philadelphians towards musical events.

These annual reports are never uninteresting, often pathetic, generally amusing. They are a very sensitive barometer of the musical atmosphere, with great depression at one end and extreme elation at the other,— with the needle always pointing to one of the opposites, never in an equilibrium of quiet content. Knowing how often and how quickly the clouds break, we cannot possibly move up and down in loyal sympathy. Like children, the good directors are either smiling with complacent self-congratulation or they are wofully trying desperate measures to prevent the worst. It was evidently an age for superlatives.

In the main there were two contrary policies. The managers saw with early foresight that the best foundation was an artistic independence. This was probably the real reason for the experiment of an "Academy" to educate members for the Society's orchestra. It was felt that the true constitution of the Society should be such that it could provide its own concerts, independent of the glamour of foreign names.

MUSIC IN PHILADELPHIA

Of course, there were financial considerations, which may have been stronger than others. The price of singers or players was even in those days fabulous. Our American cities were the last resort of worn-out "celebrities," who still sought to reap a golden harvest with the magic of their name. It was for the Society at the same time an ideal and a practical policy to rely on their own resources. It meant the production of the great master-works by concerted effort, instead of a dazzling exhibition of clever feats. In the earliest years the great desire was for oratorio. An evening of "The Creation," where the members were singers, players, and performers, was always sure of success. It was a wholesome taste, and the highest economy of means. Towards the middle of the century the oratorio seems to have lost ground. In so far as it was overshadowed by Italian opera, this was deplorable. The true successor of the oratorio was the symphony, which needed a complete orchestra. As yet, strange as it must seem, there is no record before 1840 of performances in Philadelphia of the great symphonies of Haydn, Mozart, or Beethoven. The true policy, as was constantly suggested in annual reports, was independence of virtuosi on the line of orchestral

Majgrevi Sinfonia.

A. Religion
B. Bandi Bouquires
C. Bon Cree

D. Der Heidrich
E. Brass
F. Fiddles

G. Mihnuella
g.o. Violes
h. Piva Butter

H. Bass f Contrabasso
— La Drum
ii. Cornu

i. Clarinzen
k. Flötedes
l. Smolaselowitz
Pfiffs.

MUSICAL FUND SOCIETY

concerts. In the moment of greatest achievement in the score of years before the Civil War, this highest of ideas was actually accomplished. But they were moments, and they have never been repeated. Yet in them lies the seed of promise. Somehow artistic enterprise in Philadelphia has since always suffered with a certain moral palsy, an intellectual diffidence. We have never fitted ourselves with the necessaries for musical housekeeping. We have always had to depend on foreign caterers.

In the early forties there is renewed clamor, in the managing councils, for an adjunct "school," almost as if there had never been a previous trial and failure. The "Academy" was actually re-established, with the same result as before. But, chimerical as may be the undertaking, we must sympathize earnestly with the fundamental purpose. "It is greatly to be desired," says the annual report of May, 1840, "that the taste for purely instrumental music were more generally cultivated, and that the classic and more elaborate productions of the masters of the art excited the same pleasure as is now afforded by lighter compositions. The material of which our orchestra is composed is of a sufficient

MUSIC IN PHILADELPHIA

character to produce with credit the works to which we have reference, were the public better tutored to appreciate their excellence.

"It is desirable for our Society, both on the score of economy and the permanent improvement of musical taste, that in this respect more alterations should be made in the programmes of our concerts, and a more prominent part assigned than heretofore to the orchestral department of the Society."

The taste for "lighter compositions" had come in with the later school of Italian opera, which cast aside all serious dramatic plans in the chance for languishing arias and dazzling *fioriture*. With the new music came its singers, who did not help matters with their exhibitions of highest notes and their artificial dramatic excitement. Indeed, the spirit of virtuosity infected all regions of music,—violinists, too, and pianists, as we shall see. It is now almost inconceivable to think of the old enjoyment of an evening with the simple airs of the "Creation" or of the "Seasons." That was a time of normal appreciation. Then came the good, simple programmes of overtures of Mehul, Gluck, Cherubini, or Mozart, and of plain English ballads. After the first quarter of

MUSICAL FUND SOCIETY

a century came the first draught of the new Italian brand of sparkling melody. It were vain to blame our grandfathers for this departure. It is simply one of the zigzag ways art takes in its development. In Germany the standards of true art were never overwhelmed by these Italian onsets. It is good to see how in Philadelphia the feeling for the best, for serious music soon found expression.

It was probably in fulfilment of this general purpose, and certainly in consequence of the same economic necessity, that the notice was published which we find in the newspapers on November 6, 1841:

"MUSICAL FUND SOCIETY.

" The Society have determined to substitute a series of musical soirées during the present season for the concerts heretofore given. These soirées will be five in number and will be given on the second Thursday of November, December, January, February, and March, in the Society's practising room, which has been fitted up for the purpose.

"The instrumental performances will consist of quartettes and other concerted pieces and solos; the vocal performances of songs, glees, etc., etc."

Ladies are "particularly requested" not to "wear their bonnets in the concert-room."

But the policy was not popular. It was merely the temporary recoil from the ex-

MUSIC IN PHILADELPHIA

travagant expense of the regular concerts. Indeed, during one of these winters all concerts of the Society were suspended. These troubles proved the spur which soon led to a triumphant success. They tested the sincerity of the directors and public loyalty. Recently there had been no increase of members. In 1843-44, some sixty new names appear.* So the next report is a pæan of joy, mingled with dignified self-approval, and with complacent review of the exchequer. All was well. The Society now had their cake, and ate it too. Together with an effective development of the orchestra, there is a remarkable procession of foreign genius. First comes the great Norwegian violinist. Ole Bull's first entrance is strictly characteristic of his personal quality. In the memoir, written by his widow, we read that "he received a letter from the managers of the Musical Fund Society in which they asked him to appear at their first concert of the season, and expressed the hope that he would make the terms as moderate as possible, as the object of the Society was to create a fund for the support of poor musicians."

---

* [Among them is that of the compiler, who later took a leading part.—Ed.]

OLE BULL'S SECOND CONCERT

At the
MUSICAL FUND HALL,
ON
SATURDAY EVENING, 18th JANUARY, 1845.

PROGRAMME:

PART FIRST.

I.—OVERTURE. Rossini, - - - ORCHESTRA.
II.—CONCERTO IN A. in 3 parts,
   1. ALLEGRO MAESTOSO,
   2. ADAGIO SENTIMENTALE, } composed and
   3. RONDO PASTORALE, } performed by } OLE BULL.
III.—SINFONIA. Bethovan, - - - ORCHESTRA.
IV.—NIAGARA, (Pastorale Fantasia,) composed
   and performed by - - - - OLE BULL.

PART SECOND.

I.—OVERTURE. Auber, - - - ORCHESTRA.
II.—PSALM OF DAVID, newly composed and
   performed by - - - OLE BULL.
III.—SINFONIA. Mozart, - - ORCHESTRA.
IV.—SOLITUDE OF THE PRAIRIE, composed
   and performed by - - - OLE BULL.

Grand Orchestra, under the direction of Signor LA MANNA.

TICKETS—ONE DOLLAR EACH.

☞ Doors Open at 7—Concert to commence at 8 o'clock.

A. Scott, Printer, No. 115 Chestnut street, Philadelphia.

MUSICAL FUND SOCIETY

He returned a letter of thanks, and said his only remuneration should be the honor of assisting so highly esteemed a society in its noble efforts. When they received his answer, they resolved to strike a medal in his honor, and it was presented to him at the close of the concert. It might have a grander air to tell the story in the magnificent phrases of the programme and of the report, rather than in Mrs. Bull's simple words. A special committee was appointed to prepare a gold medal with suitable emblems and inscription. John K. Kane, the vice-president, made the address of presentation on the night of the concert. Ole Bull, unlike many musical visitors in America, was in the first flush of his power. He was thirty-four years old, and had just completed his first tour of Europe. Fanny Elsler, whom he met in Hamburg, persuaded him to come to America. At this first concert in Philadelphia he played Paganini's "Carnival of Venice," and a "Quartetto" of his own, "composed for four violins and performed on one." He gave in all five concerts in Philadelphia in a fortnight. Generosity was a ruling passion with Ole Bull. In 1845 he played in New York to four thousand people, for the widows and orphans of masons. During this first visit he gave more than twenty thousand dollars to charitable and benevolent institutions. Indeed, most of his thoughts and earnings, it would seem, were spent on philanthropic enterprises, which were, unfortunately, not always successful.

Of other eminent visitors at the hall were W. V. Wallace, composer of "Maritana"; Madame Cinti Damoureau, for whom Rossini wrote special *rôles;* Artôt, the violinist; and Signor Sanguirico, the great buffo. Mr. Richard Grant White tells us* that he had rare comic power, which depended both upon his face and upon his voice. "He had a nose like Punchinello's, and the quality of his voice was also exactly like that of Mr. Punch. The sight of his queer visage and the sound of his cackling voice never failed to send laughter through an audience. He was much esteemed for his intelligence and his character." Our old friend, Henry Russell, was still giving "grand vocal entertainments."

Still in this season of 1843-44 came Madame Castellan; Signor Casella, a great cellist; and, finally, Vieuxtemps, dominant figure in violin music since Paganini. Of great merit, though less renown, were

---

* In the "Century Magazine."

MUSICAL FUND SOCIETY

Rosina Pico, contralto; and Cerillo Antognini, whose magnificent endowment of tenor voice, manly beauty, and dramatic power were marred by a strange lack of vocal control. It is said that his voice would suddenly desert him in the middle of an evening. It was a wonderful time for violinists. In the same year Ole Bull, Vieuxtemps, and Sivori were playing in the United States. Others visited the city who would now make a greater stir. It must have been the genius of the magician Paganini which pulsed in these, the chief of his apostles. We can imagine his power when we see his stamp in so reactionary a master of another instrument as Robert Schumann. With Paganini the wonders of virtuosity were legitimately expressive of a wildly passionate imagination. In his followers these means were made the end. Of them all, Ole Bull was the worst offender, we fear. Neither Vieuxtemps nor Sivori attempted such gymnastic feats as cutting the strings and performing on a single one. It is said that Vieuxtemps came unheralded on the strength of his European name; that he was disappointed and grieved with the public enthusiasm over Ole Bull. The best imitator of Paganini was undoubtedly Sivori, his only pupil, on whom he concen-

MUSIC IN PHILADELPHIA

trated all his power of instruction. But by the irony of artistic fate, the very quality which made him shine a perfect reflection of the master, meant the want of personality. The impression we get is of classic perfection of technique with a certain coldness, even affectation, of feeling.*

Despite this brilliant array, the Board of Directors were right in reporting to the Society in May, 1845, "that the past year has been chiefly remarkable for the reorganization of the orchestra . . . and its establishment, we trust permanently, upon a footing calculated to bring great credit to the Society, and to promote a sound and critical musical taste in the community.

"The performances of this orchestra during the past season have commanded the highest admiration and approval. At the second concert the orchestra performed the entire symphony of Beethoven, No. 1, in C major. The ability with which these complicated, yet expressive, harmonies were produced, and their appreciation and evident approval by one of the largest audiences ever gathered within the walls of the Musical Fund Hall, is gratifying

---

* See the sketch in Grove's "Dictionary of Music and Musicians."

MUSICAL FUND SOCIETY

evidence of advancing musical skill and taste in the community."

Turning curiously to the programme, the first to record the playing of a real master's symphony in Philadelphia, we find a modest, single-paged leaf. In largest type are Signorina Rosina Pico, Signor Antognini, and Signor Sanguirico, as if to hide the hazardous notice of "The Entire Grand Symphony of Beethoven." Wisely the latter was not allowed the test of its merits. Perhaps the wealth of singers was sugar for the pill. It looks like further precautions against a mutinous audience. The entire symphony is there, to be sure, but carefully divided through the evening in slices not too indigestible. No. 1 is first fragment of symphony, *adagio* and *allegro;* not until after four operatic *entermets* come the second and third fragments, *andante* and *minuet.* Before the fourth, *finale allegro*, there is a much-needed intermission. In the absence of written comment, we must merely wonder at the reception. Unprepared, as the audience was, by the simpler works of Haydn and Mozart, accustomed only to the frivolous overtures of Italian and French opera, the bold and serious thought of the great romanticist must have puzzled all but the musically trained. We must wonder, too, at the interpretation. But even if we had comment, there were no critics. The leader of the orchestra, who for years had taken the place of the veteran Hupfeld, was L. Meignen. It is strangely difficult to find accounts of him. At a concert in April, 1845, there is a *grand military sinfonia*, of his composition, on the concert card, entitled "A Soldier's Dream." On the third page is a long "descriptive analysis," much like a school-boy's essay. All the details of battle were, of course, to be found in the music: a notion of a "sinfonia," hard to reconcile with profound perceptions. But we may do him injustice. He certainly had the courage to bring the highest before an uncertain audience.

At the only concert of the next season, in March, 1846, the second symphony of Beethoven was given in precisely the same fragmental way. People were once for all used to short numbers. The form of lighter music must correspond with its content. It would have been presumptuous to play continuously for forty-five minutes. The rest of the programme was, for the most part, Donizetti, Meyerbeer, Vieuxtemps, and De Beriot. There was a "celebrated pianist," Leopold de Meyer, who must have been

H. VIEUXTEMPS.

CONCERT.

MUSICAL FUND SOCIETY

wonderful, for his bill was four hundred dollars.

Now, in the season 1846-47, comes the best of all. By quick evolution, the first concert has a programme of the highest modern standard. Here is the "Eroica Symphony" of Beethoven, now divided merely into two sections, beginning and ending Part I. Then there is the "Oberon" overture of Weber, and Mendelssohn's "Midsummer Night's Dream." The symphony and the Mendelssohn overture were played for the first time. On the same evening there played one of the greatest pianist-composers of the century. At least contemporary opinion would justify this praise. Henri Herz was one of those mortals who achieve at once, in the very doing, a name out of all proportion to their true value. During this time he moved quite an equal in the circle of Liszt and Chopin at Paris. His playing was prodigiously successful; his compositions always hit the instant mark of popularity. Yet when he died, a few years ago, all the world was astonished that he had been alive so long. At this concert, in December, 1846, Herz played a concerto and some Variations di Bravura of his own.

We are near the high tide of true artistic

success. From the report on the season 1847-48 the orchestra was "larger in numbers, more complete in organization, and far more perfect in execution than in any previous period."

MUSICAL FUND SOCIETY

CHAPTER XI. ENLARGEMENT OF THE HALL: THE BAZAAR: TWO GREAT PIANISTS.

THE proudest boast of the report of 1847 was, however, the alteration and improvement of the hall. "The north front of the building was extended sixteen feet, and the position of the stage was changed from the north front of the saloon to the rear or south end. The improvements were made from plans presented by N. Le Brun, architect. They were commenced June 17, and were finished on October 21, following." The change in no wise injured the acoustics; it gave a comfortable seating capacity for fifteen hundred persons. The stage was also extended.

What interests us most is the plan for paying the bill; the instant response of members to the scheme of the directors; and, above all, the enthusiastic support of the general public. It was decided that a fair be held, and that it be called "The Bazaar for the benefit of the Musical Fund Society." The hall was reserved

MUSIC IN PHILADELPHIA

from Tuesday, November 23, to Friday, December 3. It was decorated in "beautiful design."

In the newspapers a notice promised "a very extensive and elegant collection of ornamental and useful articles . . . exposed for sale by a large number of Ladies of the city and country." There was a grand promenade concert every evening in the saloon, "and numerous other wholly novel attractions presented to add brilliancy and enjoyment to the scene." On the lower floor was a museum of "valuable specimens of Art, Historical relics, and National trophies," also miscellaneous exhibitions of legerdemain, archery, an automatic trumpeter, "a perfectly acting Automatic Rope Dancer, etc., etc."

The best of the bazaar was "The Bazaar Album," a four-page paper, "devoted to the interests of the Ladies' Bazaar, for the benefit of the Musical Fund Society." Like solid houses, with perfect lines, this clear, careful type is somehow peculiarly associated with the past. And for some reason the little sheet speaks very directly of the great occasion. It is all so light in intention, so short-lived in expectation. And yet so careful is the detail, so high the standard in expression and appearance,

THE BAZAAR ALBUM.

Devoted to the interests of the Ladies' Bazaar, for the benefit of the Musical Fund Society.

PHILADELPHIA, DECEMBER 1, 1847.

Numbers One and Two.

Pray do stop and take a view,
Of my two Tables, One and Two,
Toys and Purses, rich Gold Vases,
Boxes, Dolls with pretty faces;
Nice and Ten, they talk of be Jo,
Now, only look on our side.
There's no comparison between the two.
Six in a field;—she cant come too;
Ours is going at Half a Dollar,
Do come and see, the rest will follow,
Jealousy's a most spiteful passion,
But then, just see, it is the fashion.
I must recant, the Beds at Ten
Perhaps may chance to please the men,
There on canvass sweet roses bloom,
The tables covered with rare perfume,
Slippers in grave young gentlemen's feet,
Worked in patterns, rich and neat,
And the prettiest Baby Basket,
Ready for any who may ask it,
And the most superb Chess Table,
I'ts there who do that items are able,
And as to nymphs, who do pretends
Around this stand, on every side,
Of Youth and Beauty ever can claim
Their sweet attention, you'll come again,
If bright black eyes and sunny hair
Is the spell of beauty, you'll find it here,
And these French chairs, the "beau ideal"
Of three French chairs, but there are real,
A beautiful made of stars of silk,
Some call it vulgarly, a quilt,
A toilet table, pink and white,
So beautiful, 'tis quite a sight,
Fans in bale young ladies' faces,
When Bazars would grace their faces,
Golden Tassels for the hair,
They give the head a queenly air,
Smoking Caps for handsome beaux,
Night caps, for men who love repose,
Of silk, the pattern worn by Naomi,
I fear the story's painted upon us,
But if 'tis true, they must be prime,
Better than any Anodyne,
So pray remember Number Two,
Stop and look at us, do and do.

Charity

Mr. Burke said, " There are two ways by which people may be charitable—the one by the r money,—and the other by their exertions;" still he might have added by kindness. How often has a small expression of kindness without being designed as a favor, been the germ of happiness to the longing and discouraged!! There is, moreover, a kindness of manner that is as acceptable as the wounded spirit as the quick dew to the drooping flower. The tone of voice, the expression of the eye, interpret the emotions of kindred hearts, more eloquently than mere language.

How much have these to do with our dearest affections? They are the charms of a mother's, a sister's, a lover's or a friend's society.

Marianna.
A Tale of Mexico.
BY † GABRI LA FOY.†

One afternoon in the month of June, 1843, a clipper schooner laden with cotton, was slowly ashore on a reef near Point Isabel by a " Norther." The captain soon weent to sea that without aid he could not save his cargo or vessel, and as going ashore in his boat, he found a cluster of wooden buildings, occupied by the Mexican Custom House Officers, at Point Isabel was then a port of entry.

With the aid of the Mexicans his cargo was soon safely landed, and to obtain a remittance of the heavy duty thereof, the captain set out with a Mexican guide to Matamoras. On arriving he was imprisoned and his cargo and vessel confiscated, for landing without permission from Matamoras !

In prison he remained for weeks, but suddenly he heard something strike the grating of his cell, he rushes forward and beholds the face of a beautiful Mexican girl regarding him attentively—soon a cord is thrown him, he catches it, and drew up a basket filled with food and clothing. Returning them in his cell, he allowed the basket to descend, and with tender eyes expressed his thanks,—receiving and evening did the young girl appear, again he receives fresh sustenance, and new flowers telling in their simple but beautiful language her love of him.

Days, weeks rolled on, he was yet prisoner, and that gentle one was ever with him.

In the sad hour of his prison, the thoughts of home, kindred, mother, sister, all, and when at eve his kind and attentive friend was near, he thought but of love for one whose name he knew not, one whose very language he spake not—but she loved him—this and this only supported him.

But another morn and eve have passed, and the curse out—hark! what means that sudden cry? whence is that fearful explosion in the air ? what strange concussion shakes his prison walls ! the cry Americans! Americans!

Can it be his countrymen ! Yes, these dearly as they, those horrid arms, all speak that American arms are here about to free him. Fort Brown is speaking with its iron messengers, and soon d t captives will be free.

And that ! ah where is she ?

The air is still, the cannon cease their roar, his prison door grates on its hinges, he comes forth free, his countrymen surround him; Matamoras is taken!

His eyes run o'er the crowd who throng around him, 'tis she ! he pushes all aside, and clasps her to his heart.

She and early despatched a messenger to the town Taylor, and he demanded he was an American, and American Lands led by his unknown guardian have freed him.

Need we say that ere long he was united to one who had for him left all, dared all, braved all. And attached to the army he has rendered important service, and with a happy Mariana, thanks the " Norther" for his landing on Mexican soil.

This is on his own, the parties are known to the writer—and such is woman's love!

On St. Patrick's eve, the steerage passengers on board of one of the packets, then about midway between the port and Liverpool, were enjoying a convivial entertainment. The President, a native of the Emerald Isle, being called upon for a toast, gave, " *Here's to the land we live in.*"

History of Poison.

When Noel planted the first plant, he entered (Satan approached and said, « I will name you, charming plant " He quickly brought three menues, a lamb, a lion, and a hog, and killed them one after another, near the root. The vessel of the blood of these animals penetrated it, and in each visible in its growth. When a man drinks the goblet of wine, he is then agreeable, gentle and friendly. That is the nature of the lamb. When he drinks two, he is a lion, and rages, " Who is like me !" He then talks of stupendous things.—When he drinks more his senses forsake him, and at length he wallows in the mire. Need it be said that he then resembles the hog !

Jenny Lind's Return to Lablache.

On the occasion of M'lle Lind's refund rehearsal at the Opera House, the celebrated Lablache was so delighted with her singing that he came up to her and said enthusiastically, " Give me your hand ; every note in your voice is a pearl!" " Give me your hair," was the reply of the fair singer ; and then putting it up to her mouth, and giving one of her incomparable roulades, " here," said she, " is a ht full of pearls for you." Apropos, we see that " the nightingale" has lately made an engagement with her Majesty's Theatre.

Malleable Glass.

Professor Bohmann has invented the gun cotton, is stated to have discovered malleable glass. *Marquders papier mache* (paper paste) transparent by stewing it to undergo a certain metamorphosis, which he calls catalysis, for want of a more intelligent term. He makes of the new paper, window panes, vases, bottles, &c., perfectly impermeable to water, and which may be dropped on the ground without breaking, and are quite transparent.

The Gourd and the Palm Leaf.

A gourd wound itself round a lofty palm, and in a few weeks shined in the very top. " How old may'st thou be ?" asked the new comer. " About a hundred years," was the answer. " A hundred years and no taller ? Only look. I have grown as tall as you in fewer days than you can count years." " I know that well," replied the palm. " Every summer of my life a gourd has climbed up round me, as proud as thou art and as short-lived as thou wilt be."

Acceptances and Bills.

During the late commercial crisis, a committeman merchant, who was some thousands short, stood in the portico of the Exchange, in a brown study, from which he was awakened by the chirping of two sparrows which flew near. " Happy creatures," said he, " you have no acceptances to pay." " No," said a lean broker, who had money to loan on certain securities, and at certain rates, " but they have bills to provide for."

The heart wounds which are inflicted by our fellow-creatures are yet in their ; these which we receive in dispensations of Almighty wisdom and the course of nature, are remedial and assuasive. There are some fluids which must be punctured before they can repose kindly; and there are hearts which require an analogous process.

MUSICAL FUND SOCIETY

that it somehow deserves its accidental preservation. Almost half is filled with persuasive verses about the various tables. There is a very slim editorial department. One of the burning topics is the weather. Another, on "The Opera," says: "The musical world has taken it into its head to be delighted with the singing of Madame Bishop, etc., etc." A third tells us that "Mr. Dempster, the popular ballad singer, is in the city, and is drawing throngs of delighted listeners to his pleasing and instructive entertainments. He is undoubtedly the best English ballad singer of the day." Then there is a funny, old-fashioned plaint of a newly-married "Peter Pliant."

The bazaar was a very great success. After it was over, there was announced in the newspapers a "Bazaar Ball in honor of the Ladies, superintendents of the Tables at the Musical Fund Bazaar. This Grand Ball will take place on Thursday, December 23rd, 1847, at the Musical Fund Hall."

"An elegant supper, including wines," was promised. We are prepared for the fine humor of the board in its next report: "Never before have they been able to present the general affairs of the Institution in a more flourishing condition. The alterations of the Hall and improvements have been completed, and the additional accommodations have produced the most advantageous results."

"To the ladies . . . grateful acknowledgments" are given at ceremonious length. "The result of this devotion was a clear receipt of $5000." The sum surpassed all earlier attempts, and paid for the greater share of the expenses of the alterations.

The remaining history of the Society down to the clouding shadows of the coming war is outwardly brilliant with the visits of singers and players, who, more than mere kings of a day, had something of the quality of perfection which leaves a lasting mark on the memory of man. Besides the Brignolis, the Grisis, the Marios, besides Lagrange, Alboni, and Hensler, there was a Lind; above all there was Sontag. Finally, this resplendent sunset of the Society was further enriched by the appearance of one of the great pianists of history. The comments of the time on Gottschalk's playing, the recorded impression of his personality, allow us no hesitation in giving him this rank. There is no doubt that in many ways he lowered his art to the level of clownish exhibtion. Yet, withal, he had the courage to introduce

MUSICAL FUND SOCIETY

the unknown music of Chopin and other romanticists. His influence on the music of this country, measured merely in power, without regard to quality, was far greater than that of any other virtuoso. In his manner of playing, in what are called his own compositions, which are mere arrangements of well-known melodies, he completely dominated all taste. Even to-day, forty years afterwards, in quiet villages, like lonely cavities where rain-pools linger, it is Gottschalk's music, with his portrait on the cover, that still reigns supreme among "fashionable pieces." And then, too, he had the disadvantage of being an American. He made a far stronger mark in this country than did Henri Herz. His personality was broader: he approached nearer to original creation.

But it was largely a mere outward splendor. Behind the scenes, with the directors over their annual reports while these magnificent concerts are progressing, everything is really going wrong. The "professors" will not come to rehearse, and the orchestra rapidly goes down. With all their popularity, singers were always a losing investment, generally in proportion to their greatness. The success of the new Germania Orchestra seemed to show that the public were eager for good performance of instrumental music. But, while the purpose of the Society was beneficial to professional musicians, there must have been too slight a present reward to induce faithful attendance.

All of this did not, of course, affect the financial condition of the Society. The income from rent of hall and rooms had increased continuously, until in May, 1857, the board reported: "All the incumbrances upon the property of the Society have been removed, and it is without debt." This was, too, the year when an unusual competition began with the completion of Jayne's Hall and of the Academy of Music. "The trouble lay purely in the 'musical department,' which betrayed its inability for self-support." In reviewing causes, the report continues later: "In the early part of the career of the Society, the giving of concerts and productions of classic compositions, such as the 'Creation,' directed as it freely was by the resident musical ability of the day, and aided by the amateur force under its control, was not only a means of cultivating and diffusing taste for music but was also a source of revenue. Subsequently the engagement of such passenger talent as came within the

MUSICAL FUND SOCIETY

reach of the officers, enabled them to give attractive and generally lucrative concerts. But for several years past the enormous demands of these persons have rendered it difficult to procure such aid, and often impossible except at a heavy loss. In short, the attractive and often elevated character of the opera companies which appear among us, have given a style to public performances with which it is impossible for the Society to compete."

It might have been said, however, that the question of self-support in the musical department was a minor one, when there was a permanent fund destined for its assistance. After all, these are old lamentations, ringing out their yearly plaint on an accustomed tune. Probably, but for the Civil War, the former efforts would have been renewed with the former success.

We have hurried ahead of our glorious period, fearful that it is too good to last. Before us are still the greatest of all who have yet sung or played. All so far has been prelude: now comes the natural climax. At the worst, *plaudite, amici; comedia finita est.* It is something to have held such an array of guests, if the house does tumble into decay.

MUSIC IN PHILADELPHIA

CHAPTER XII. THE AGE OF SONG: SONTAG AND LIND: THE FUTURE.

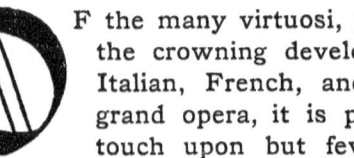

OF the many virtuosi, product of the crowning development of Italian, French, and German grand opera, it is possible to touch upon but few. These great soloists are, pathetically, like unwilling members of a grand chorus, most of whom, at our distance, with all the shower of adjectives, look very like each other. Some few hold our glance with an unusual charm.

Not more than the accustomed numbers stand out as the final chosen *prime* and *primi*.

In 1850 Jenny Lind gave two concerts at the hall. But there is no trace of her singing at any of the regular concerts of the Society. Her terms were certainly discouraging. But in the following May the treasurer reports a generous gift from her, of four hundred dollars, to the funds of the Society. Her name was, of course, promptly enrolled among the honorary

Musical Fund Hall.

MADAME HENRIETTE SONTAG'S Grand Extra Concert

ASSISTED BY

CESARE BADIALI,   M. CARL ECKERT,
Sig. G. POZZOLINI,   LUIGI ROCCO,
PAUL JULIEN,   ALFRED JAELL,

AND THE

GERMANIA MUSICAL SOCIETY,

On SATURDAY Evening, October 30th.

CARD.

MADAME HENRIETTE SONTAG, desirous of imparting to this, her **LAST** Concert, unusual splendor and brilliancy, will introduce,

FOR THE FIRST TIME
CONCERTED OPERATIC PIECES!

Which will be executed by the Grand Combination of Eminent Artists who have assisted her at their previous Concerts in this City.

PROGRAMME.

PART I.

1. OVERTURE..."Der Freyschutz,".................. WEBER
   THE GERMANIA MUSICAL SOCIETY.
2. DUET........From "I Puritani,"................. BELLINI
   SIGS. BADIALI and ROCCO.
3. CAVATINA..."O Luce di Questa," Linda di Chamounix, DONIZETTI
   MADAME HENRIETTE SONTAG.
4. PIANO FORTE..."Carnival of Venice,"............ JAELL
   ALFRED JAELL.
5. DUET....From "Linda di Chamounix,"............. DONIZETTI
   MADAME HENRIETTE SONTAG
   And SIGNOR POZZOLINI.

PART II.

6. OVERTURE...."Merry Wives of Windsor,"......... NICOLAI
   THE GERMANIA MUSICAL SOCIETY.
7. BALLAD...."Katy Darling,".....................
   MADAME HENRIETTE SONTAG.
8. ROMANZA....From "I Normani in Parag[i],"...... MERCADANTE
   SIGNOR BADIALI.
9. DUET   "The Music Lesson,"................... FIORAVANTI
   MADAME HENRIETTE SONTAG
   And SIGNOR ROCCO.
10. VIOLIN...." Souvenir de Bellini,"............. ARTOT
    PAUL JULIEN.
11. QUARTET....From "Lucia di Lammermoor,"........ DONIZETTI
    MADAME HENRIETTE SONTAG,
    And SIGS. BADIALI, POZZOLINI, and ROCCO.
12. FINALE....Orchestral,.........................
    THE GERMANIA MUSICAL SOCIETY.

Conductor . . . . CARL ECKERT.
Leader . . . . CARL BERGMANN.

Admission - - $1, $2, and $3.

Tickets and Seats to be had at Lee & Walker's Music Store.

The Chickering Grand Piano, used at this Concert, has been kindly loaned by Mr. E. L. Walker, corner of Fifth and Chesnut Streets.

Doors Open at 7.   Commence at 8 o'clock.

Brown, Printer, Ledger Building, Phila.

MUSICAL FUND SOCIETY

members. With other pre-eminent singers of the time the Society had closer relations. The story of Madame Sontag's reception suggests at once the prestige of the lady, and the fine attitude, of *noblesse oblige*, of our Society. They were alive to their duty as representatives of the city. A committee was given power to make arrangements at a cost of three hundred dollars. In the formal correspondence that followed, Sontag, through her agent, offered to sing gratuitously for the benefit of Musical Fund Society. Her approach to Philadelphia was conceived in the form of an ovation. On Wednesday, October 13, 1852, a steamboat was chartered for Burlington, New Jersey, to meet Madame Sontag, arriving by rail from New York. The lady was escorted by the committee on board, where she was received by the venerable George Campbell, secretary of the Society. He advanced and addressed her in these words: "Honored madame! The Musical Fund Society, of Philadelphia, desirous to express the high estimation in which they and the kindred associations of this city hold your character as an artist and lady, have made arrangements to meet you here for the purpose of welcoming and escorting you to Philadelphia. The fame of your talents and your virtues have long ago preceded you, and the opportunity of meeting personally one who has for many years occupied so distinguished a rank in the musical world, and contributed so much to dignify and exalt the divine art you profess, affords us the most sincere pleasure. We therefore gladly welcome your appearance among us, and hope your visit may be in all respects agreeable to yourself."

Perhaps the best proof at this day of the lady's artistic sincerity was the contrasting simplicity of her reply: "Sir, I am totally unprepared for the kindness thus shown to me. It is as delightful as it is touching and flattering to my feelings. Accept, sir, my heartfelt thanks, where it will ever be deeply engraved. Thanks, thanks, dear sir! to you and your noble Society." One who was present tells of a "splendid collation" that was served. A band played, and German musical societies sang choruses. The boat stopped at Browning's Ferry, Shackamaxon Street, where Madame Sontag, her husband, Count Rossi, Paul Julien, and Louis C. Madeira landed and drove to Jones's Hotel, on Chestnut Street, in order to avoid the crowd at the Walnut Street wharf. Madame Sontag acknowledged with much fervor the pleasure which the

MUSICAL FUND SOCIETY

reception gave her. Those who were present speak of it as memorable.

Sontag's first concert was given on the next evening at Musical Fund Hall. With her sang Cesare Badiale, and played Paul Julien, violinist, and Alfred Jaell, pianist. There was, too, the orchestra of the new Germania Musical Society, and a Carl Eckert, conductor from the Italian opera at Paris, who led the former. The programme is not interesting. Best of all is Weber's overture to "Euryanthe." Sontag sang, of known music, an aria from "Sonnambula," "Di Questa Anima" from "Linda," and "Home, Sweet Home." Descriptions of the scene at each night are dazzling. "When Sontag first appeared," we are told, "a solemn stillness ensued, as if an immortal had descended." Sontag was then at least fifty years old. The public called for a new series of concerts, which were given with sustained success.

Before us lies the original letter which Sontag wrote to the president of the Society before returning to New York. It gives her "most cordial thanks" for her "kind and sympathetic reception." But it is not as good as her first little speech. What was most important was her offer to give a concert, with the help of her "professional assistants," in behalf of the Society. On its programme were the same songs for Sontag, except the aria from "Sonnambula." Instead, Sontag and a Signor Rocco sang an unimportant duet.

In the fall of 1853, Sontag sang in concerts; she also produced some operas at the National Amphitheatre, on Chestnut Street below Ninth. On a Saturday in October she gave a free performance to the girls of the Normal School, who loaded her with flowers. It took four large clothes-baskets to carry them away; but she would not leave one behind. The house was crowded, the stage filled with children on both sides. Sontag was as much delighted as were the children.

Coming, as she did, with a bevy of wonderful singers, Sontag seems to have left with her hearers the sense of *ne plus ultra*. Closely rivalling the musical admiration was the personal regard which she commanded. Beethoven spoke as true seer, when he said, "I predict for her a glorious career; for she has heart as well as voice."

There can, however, be no comparison between the public interest in Sontag and the rage over Lind. Undoubtedly there was a striking conjunction of various ele-

MUSICAL FUND SOCIETY

ments. The picturesque story of her youth, great personal power, and the first campaign of modern advertising, sprung upon an unwitting public. At least two of these traits have nothing to do with the art of singing. But they conspired to stir the world like nothing before or since in the world of art.

Twenty-five thousand people are said to have welcomed Jenny Lind at the wharf in New York. At an auction sale for choice of seats at her first concert, two hundred and twenty-five dollars was bid by a hatter, who won fortune by the venture of a moment. The receipts of the first evening were $30,000. In Philadelphia the sum paid for first choice of seats was six hundred and twenty-five dollars. Musical Fund Hall, where the first concerts were given, was abandoned for an amphitheatre, once a circus, called Maretzek's Opera House. In Washington the President called on Jenny Lind; eminent statesmen paid her distinguished honor. At one concert, when Lind was singing "Hail Columbia," the great Webster, whose patriotism was boiling over, involuntarily rose and added his bass to the chorus, to the delight of Lind and the audience. At the close the *impromptu concertanti* bowed and courtesied with increasing insistence, while the audience applauded like enchanted children.

Such a triumph cannot be laughed away as mere imaginary admiration without the element of personal power.

In this dazzling light it is hard to see the individual beauty of lesser stars without a special effort of historical magnifying. Lind's visit was in 1850; Sontag came in 1852. On the 1st of December, 1855, the Musical Fund Society gave its eighty-second concert with Miss Hensler, Signor Brignoli, and Gottschalk; in the following April Brignoli sang again with Madame La Grange and Signor Amodio. Finally Mario and Grisi appeared in Philadelphia in opera and concert early in 1855. All of these are peers of the realm of one province of a great art. Each in turn may seem brightest and best. The difference is largely in the subjective temperament of the hearer. One writer tries to distinguish the charm of Grisi: " Malibran was more startling in her impulses; Viardot more intensely dramatic; Jenny Lind more sensational with her four high notes; Sontag more brilliant. But for the presentation of a part in its entireness; for the embodiment of powerful emotion, combined with beauty of person, richness and roundness of voice, with the power of

MUSICAL FUND SOCIETY

exercising a potent spell over a vast audience, Grisi has never been surpassed." Her husband was Giuseppe Mario, son of the Marchese di Candia. Caught in a political scrape, he was reluctantly persuaded to make a trade of his song. Some of his power lay in physical beauty, and in a distinction that may have been associated with his gentle birth.

The poet Willis, hearing Grisi in "Anna Bolena," wrote the lines:

> "When the rose is brightest,
>   Its bloom will soonest die;
> When burns the meteor brightest,
>   'Twill vanish from the sky!
> If death but wait until delight
>   O'errun the heart like wine,
> And break the cup when brimming quite,
>   I die;—for thou hast poured to-night
>   The last drop into mine."

Of all the singers Elise Hensler rose highest in the measure of worldly station. A Boston girl of poor parents, the friend of Longfellow, she was married to a prince, at one time King of Portugal, who, it is said, refused the throne of Spain in loyalty to his wife.

Newspaper criticisms, to give them a flattering name, somehow improve with age. Undiscriminating as they are in description or expression, they have the virtue of spontaneous opinion, uttered before reflection has cooled the emotion. They have somewhat the value, in point of evidence, of certain declarations which in law are admitted by reason of a close relation to the incident of which they speak. There is a yellow, old comment on the singing of La Grange, which details her various perfections and makes excuses for the seeming coldness of Philadelphia audiences.

Another bit of print may, unwittingly, console us to-day for what we have thought an unheard-of wrong-doing of *impresarios*.

"ITALIAN OPERA.

"A brilliant audience was assembled last evening, solely to hear Rossini's lovely opera of the *Barber of Seville*. One act of it was done better than it was ever done here, Madame Lagrange making a more admirable *Rosina* than we have ever had, while Morelli's *Figaro* was most excellent, Brignoli's *Almaviva* much better than we expected, Gasparoni's *Don Basilio* very good, and as for Signor Rovere, he was irresistibly droll as *Dr. Bartolo*, and appeared in unusually good voice. Imagine the surprise of the audience, then, when, at the fall of the curtain, the stage manager appeared and announced that, owing to the sudden hoarseness of Signor Rovere, the rest of the opera could not be performed, but two acts of the *Puritani* would be given in its stead. Nobody believed in this sudden hoarseness, and there were plenteous hisses among the re-

MUSICAL FUND SOCIETY

sponses to the manager's announcement. It was soon discovered that the 'sudden hoarseness' had been provided for beforehand; the female choristers, dressed for *I Puritani*, had been seen by those in the side boxes, early in the evening; Miss Hensler and Signor Amodio were on hand for the *Puritani*, and scenery, dresses, and music were all so ready for the change of opera, that one could not fail to see in it something more than mere coincidence. But with a remarkable good humor, the audience submitted to the trick, and listened patiently to Miss Hensler's pretty singing of some of Elvira's music and to the noisy duo by Amodio and Morelli. That, however, which reconciled them to the unwarrantable and unnecessary change of performance was the marvellous singing of Madame Lagrange, in a Hungarian air with variations, and in her own St. Petersburg polka aria, which were kindly given between the bits of *I Puritani*. But for this, half the audience would probably have left in disgust at the trick practised upon them. To-night *Semiramide* is *promised*, and to-morrow night *Norma*. It is impossible to say whether . . . "

Here the column cuts us off abruptly; but it is not hard to guess the rest.

Almost with equal abruptness our history closes. There was, indeed, an ominous series of mournful losses. A number of the prominent founders drop away in a group. Chief of them is Benjamin Cross, who died in March, 1857. In quick succession the Society loses John K. Kane, the first secretary, untiring in founding and guiding the early venture; his successor, George Campbell; and the vice-president, Elhanan W. Keyser. The board, in annual report, utter their sense of the high worth of the departed colleagues in sincerest words.

Yet there is no reason to doubt that, but for the darkening troubles of the nation, the Society would have continued and advanced in its career. No single obstacle arose (like the competition of other halls) which could not have been met with moderate effort.

Until lately it seemed that a cause of temporary suspension had been allowed, by passive inertia, permanently to end the musical work of the Society. Signs of new enterprise are given the highest surety of success in the history of the past. The same strain of English musicians, which we have called peculiar to Philadelphia, has in later years produced, among others, one who has achieved the highest place in the highest work of the art. Where there was one German master, there are now ten,—at least of equal ability, some of creative power.

Of the elements of high development of musical life, all are now present in greater measure than in the best years of the

SECOND
GRAND CONCERT
OF
SIGNORINA ADELINA

PATTI,

The Musical Phenomenon!

MAURICE STRAKOSCH

Respectfully informs his Friends, and the Public in general, that he has engaged

SIGNORINA ADELINA PATTI,
Not yet Eight Years Old,
The Most Wonderful Vocalist of the Age!
CALLED

LA PETITE JENNY LIND.

This Extraordinary Phenomenon sings with the most astonishing perfection, purity of style, and incomprehensible ease, the Bravura Pieces of

MALIBRAN,   **MADAME ALBONI,**
PASTA,   **CATHERINE HAYES,**
JENNY LIND,   **ANNA BISHOP,**
MADAME SONTAG,   AND **TERESA PARODI,**

Exactly as they are composed, or with such changes as are used by the above named famous Artists.

SIGNORINA ADELINA PATTI
Will give her SECOND GRAND CONCERT, on

Thursday Evening, Sept. 23d, 1852,
AT THE

MUSICAL FUND HALL,
On which occasion she will be assisted by

MISKA HAUSER,
The Great Violinist, and

MAURICE STRAKOSCH,
The Eminent Pianist and Composer.

MUSICAL FUND SOCIETY

Musical Fund Society,—all save one, which was the underlying quality of the old success: a hearty union of all the musical forces of the city. With it must come confidence, instead of the old bane of self-doubt. Plans for the special pleasure of a limited class have no place in such a union. The rich must see the musical want of the poor. Providing for these, they will themselves enjoy the highest gifts of the art. It is still the old question of concentration of forces upon serious concerted instrumental music as against the frivolous enchantment of operatic vanities. The final fruit must be independent equipment for the enjoyment of the great master-works of music.

MUSIC IN PHILADELPHIA

LIST OF MEMBERS OF THE MUSICAL FUND SOCIETY AND OF OFFICERS, WITH THE DATE OF TENURE, ELECTED BETWEEN 1820 AND 1858.

Abadie, Hilarian.
Abbott, Robert, M.D.
Abercrombie, Rev. J.
Adams, Henry.
Adams, Martha.
Adams, R. W.
Adams, Thomas.
Adamson, James.
Aiken, Joseph.
Alexander, Charles.
Alexander, Samuel.
Allen, James.
Allen, J. B. A.
Allen, Solomon.
Allen, William.
Anderson, J.
Anderson, James.
Anderson, William V.
Andrade, Joseph.
André, William.
Andrews, Henry W.
Andrews, John.
Andrews, R.
Anerim, James H.

Anners, Robert M.
Ardley, Alexander.
Ash, Joshua P.
Ashmead, J.
Ashton, John.
Asson, Thomas S.
Astley, Thomas, Manager.
Atherton, Humphrey.
Atwood, John H.
Avignone, Antonio.
Aykrod, James.
Ayres, R. M. R.

Babcock, H.
Bache, Franklin, M.D.
Bacon, Allyn.
Bacon, George.
Bacon, Josiah.
Badarague, J.
Badarague, Thos., Jr.
Baker, Henry S.
Baker, Isaac F.
Baker, William J.
Baldwin, M. W.

MUSICAL FUND SOCIETY

Baldwin, S.
Ballock, Joseph, M.D.
Bancker, Charles G.
Barclay, B. S.
Barclay, C. B.
Barclay, John.
Barker, James N., Manager.
Barnes, John, M.D.
Barnes, John H., Manager.
Barnett, Joseph S., Manager.
Barrabino, E.
Barrington, Charles.
Barrow, James.
Barton, E. P.
Barton, Francis.
Barton, J. Rhea, M.D.
Barry, Edward.
Barry, Joseph.
Barry, Joseph B.
Bastert, George.
Bauersachs, Louis C.
Bayard, Charles S.
Bazley, Charles W.
Beale, Matthew L.
Beck, Charles.
Beck, Charles F., M.D.
Beck, Harvey.
Beck, Henry.
Beck, H. Paul.
Beck, John.
Beck, Levi.
Beck, Jas. Madison.
Beck, William.

Beck, William C.
Beckett, Henry.
Bedell, Rev. Gregory T.
Beetz, John F.
Bell, James.
Bell, John, M.D.
Benners, Henry B.
Benners, James.
Benson, Alex'r, Manager.
Benson, D. P.
Benson, Gustavus.
Bernadon, J. B.
Bernhart, Louis F.
Besson, Louis A.
Bethell, Robert.
Bethune, Rev. George W.
Beyer, G. T., Manager.
Beyland, Joseph.
Biddle, Clement, Jr.
Biddle, Col. Clement C.
Biddle, James.
Biddle, Nicholas.
Biddle, William F.
Biddle, William M.
Billé, Thomas.
Billington, Geo., Manager.
Bingham, William.
Binny, John.
Binney, Horace.
Birch, Wm. Y., Manager.
Birckhead, Pollard E.
Bird, James M., Director.
Bird, John D.
Bispham, Samuel.
Bispham, William.

MUSIC IN PHILADELPHIA

Blackiston, Mrs. W. C.
Blagg, John.
Blake, George E.
Blake, J. R., M.D.
Blanchard, William.
Blanchorn, Irenæus.
Blaney, Miss.
Blight, Charles.
Blight, George.
Blight, Peter.
Blight, William S.
Boggs, James.
Bohlen, Henry.
Bohlen, John.
Bohlen, John, Jr.
Bolden, George.
Boller, Henry J., Director.
Bomeisler, M.
Bond, James M., M.D.
Bonnaffon, Anthony.
Boocock, John.
Borie, A. E.
Borie, Charles L.
Borrekeus, Henry P., Manager, Director.
Boulton, John.
Bowen, John.
Boyd, William.
Boyer, C. A.
Boyle, Wm. V., Manager.
Bradford, J. H., M.D.
Breck, Samuel.
Breiter, A. K.
Bremer, John L.
Brenan, E. H.
Brenan, M. E., Director.
Brinton, Miss C.
Brock, John.
Brolaskey, Dr.
Broom, Jas. M., Manager, Counsellor.
Brown, B.
Brown, Charles J.
Brown, David P.
Brown, G. H.
Brown, G. W.
Brown, Henry A.
Brown, John.
Brown, N. B., Counsellor.
Browne, Miss Augusta.
Browne, H. A.
Bryan, S. Harvey.
Buck, C. N.
Bujac, J. Lachassé.
Bulkley, Charles.
Bulkley, J. H.
Bunker, James.
Bunting, Thomas H.
Burd, Albert Gallatin.
Burd, Edward S.
Burke, Mrs.
Burnett, E. S.
Burnett, J. G.
Burrows, Dr.
Butcher, Thomas G.
Butcher, Washington.
Butler, John.
Butler, Pierce, Director, 1854-55.

MUSICAL FUND SOCIETY

Cabell, J. C. B.
Cadwalader, George.
Caldwell, D.
Caldwell, Edmund B.
Caldwell, S.
Camac, William M.
Campbell, Colin.
Campbell, George, Manager; Sec'y, 1827-56.
Campbell, Quintin, Jr.
Cantor, Samuel.
Caravadossi.
Carazo, John.
Cardini, Signor.
Carey, Henry S.
Carey, Matthew.
Carl, W.
Carlile, Joseph C.
Carll, Rev. Maskell W.
Carr, Benjamin, Manager, Director.
Carr, Thomas, Director.
Carson, Henry, Manager.
Carswell, M. S.
Carter, William S.
Carusi, G.
Carusi, L.
Carusi, S.
Casey, W. M.
Cash, Andrew D.
Cassin, John.
Castor, Jesse G.
Catlin, George.
Chaloner, W.
Chamberlain, William.
Chancellor, Wharton.
Chapman, Nathaniel, M.D.
Chardon, Wm. Rawle.
Charnock, John.
Chester, Henry, Counsellor.
Christie, Wm.
Churchman, W. H.
Churr, Jacob, Jr.
Clapier, Fortune.
Clark, B. W.
Clark, John C.
Clark, John W.
Clark, J. Y.
Clarkson, Charles.
Clay, Joseph A., Counsellor.
Clemens, Benjamin S.
Clemens, George.
Clemson, Thomas.
Coates, John R.
Cochran, John.
Cochran, J. Harvey.
Cohen, D. J.
Cole, Isaac P.
Comrick, Dr.
Cookman, Frank.
Coombs, Gilbert A.
Cooper, Francis.
Cooper, George B.
Cooper, S. P.
Cooper, Thomas.
Cope, E. R.
Cope, F. S.
Cope, John E.

MUSIC IN PHILADELPHIA

Copper, T.
Corbin, Francis P.
Corfield, Edward D.
Cornelius, C.
Cornelius, Robert.
Cortetz, F. A.
Cowitzky.
Cowperthwaite, J. W.
Cox, George W.
Cox, Isaac N.
Cox, John.
Cox, Mrs. John.
Coxe, Alexander S.
Coxe, William S.
Craig, G. S.
Craig, James.
Craig, William.
Craige, G. S.
Crease, Charles J.
Crease, W. S.
Creighton, Robert.
Cresson, John M.
Crissy, James, Manager.
Crosby, Thomas.
Cross, Benjamin, Director.
Cross, B. Carr, Director.
Crozier, J. G.
Cuesta, Leandro de la.
Cunnington, W. P.
Curdwell, H. B.
Cuthrall, Charles E., Manager.
Cuthrall, Charles S.
Cuyler, Theodore, Manager, Counsellor.

Dallas, Capt. A. J.
Dallett, Elijah.
Dallett, Henry C.
Dallett, John.
Dannenberg, Charles.
Darley, F. T. S.
Darley, John.
Darley, W. H. W., Director.
Darrach, William, M.D.
Darrainville, Henry.
Davenport, W.
David, J. T., Director.
Davids, Hugh.
Davidson, Robert B., Manager.
Davis, Armon.
Davis, Justinian F.
Davis, J. M.
Davis, M., M.D.
Davis, Mrs. M.
Davis, Miss M.
Davis, Col. S. B.
Dawson, E. B.
De Billé, Torben.
De Bree, John B.
Deland, Thorndike.
Delprat, John C.
De Luce, Nathaniel.
De Luce, Mrs. N.
Demmé, Rev. Charles.
Denckla, Paul.
Denman, Matthew B.
Dennison, George.
Desilver, Miss E.

MUSICAL FUND SOCIETY

Desilver, Robert.
De Silver, Thomas.
Dessaigne, E.
De Wees, Miss Adaline.
Dewees, Hardman P.
Dewees, Theodore.
De Wees, Wm. S., M.D., President, 1820–38.
Dick, William.
Dickel, William.
Dickson, J. N.
Dickson, Levi.
Dietz, A. R.
Dietz, Rudolph.
Dillingham, W. S.
D'Invilliers, C.
Dittrich, W.
Donaldson, Miss M.
Donnell, J. C.
Dougherty, J. L.
Dougherty, Lewis.
Doughty, J.
Douredoure, B.
Drake, A., M.D.
Draper, Edmund.
Draper, William.
Dreyfous, S.
Drexel, Francis M.
Drexel, Joseph W.
Drinker, William W.
Drown, W. A., Jr.
Drysdale, William.
Duane, William J.
Du Bois, Louis P., Manager.
Dufour, George.
Duhring, Henry.
Dulles, Joseph H., Jr.
Dumonter, Miss Jane.
Duncan, Benjamin.
Duncan, T. O.
Dundas, James.
Dunham, Manager.
Dunglison, Robley, M.D., Manager; Vice - President, 1850–53, 1855–56; President, 1853–54, 1856–69.
Dunglison, William J.
Duponceau, Peter S.
Dupuy, Rev. C. M.
Durand, E.
Durand, John.
Durney, Tobias M.
Duval, Lewis.
Dyer, Samuel.
Dyke, Phineas.
Dyke, Ph. B.

Earle, George W.
Earp, Randall.
Eberlé, F. E.
Eberle, Jacob.
Eberle, John, M.D.
Eckert, George.
Edwards, J. G.
Edwards, Thomas J.
Eisenbrey, Philip.
Ellis, Thomas J.
Ellmaker, Levi.

MUSIC IN PHILADELPHIA

Elton, Mrs. A.
Ely, John, Jr.,
Emerick, George.
Emerson, Gouverneur, M.D., Physician.
Emlen, Miss Deborah.
Emlen, George.
Engles, Joseph P.
Engles, Rev. William M.
English, Gustavus.
Erringer, J. L.
Erwin, Robert.
Etting, Benjamin.
Evans, Charles H.
Evens, Whitton.

Farnum, James A.
Farr, George W.
Farrouihl, Andrew, Manager.
Fassitt, Wallace.
Fell, Reese D.
Fenton, W. C.
Ferguson, Peter.
Fest, Frederick.
Field, John W.
Field, Samuel.
Finley, Anthony.
Fiot, A., Director.
Fisher, Joseph, Director, Manager.
Fisher, Rodney.
Fisher, Sidney George.
Fitch, S. S.
Fitzgerald, Thomas.

Fletcher, Thomas.
Fleur, Charles.
Fontages, M.
Forsyth, William T.
Fort, Louis C.
Foster, Joseph H.
Fowle, Jonathan, Jr.
Fox, George.
Frailey, J. W.
Frank, J.
Frazer, Miss Eliza.
Frazer, John F.
Frazer, Persifor.
Frederick, J. L.
Freeman, Henry G.
Freytag, Daniel C.
Fry, Edward P.
Fry, John H.
Fry, Joseph R., Director.
Fry, William.
Fuller, Oliver.
Fuss, John.

Gallagher, Daniel.
Gandiehand, P.
Gardner, Sidney.
Garrett, William E.
Garrigues, Wm. H.
Garrison, Joseph.
George, Joseph.
Getze, F. A.
Gibbs, A.
Gibson, D.
Gibson, Hon. John B.
Gillaspie, Mrs.

MUSICAL FUND SOCIETY

Gilles, Mrs. Ann.
Gilles, P., Director.
Gillingham, C. J.
Gillingham, W. H., M.D.
Gilpin, Henry D., Counsellor.
Gobrecht, C.
Goddard, Mrs. John.
Good, Cyrus J., Manager.
Gording, Miss.
Goucher, William D.
Graff, Charles, Manager.
Graff, Christopher.
Graff, Frederick.
Graff, Jacob.
Graham, John, Director.
Graham, Peter.
Graham, W. Hicks.
Grant, Joseph P.
Gratz, Joseph.
Gray, Miss Mary B.
Gray, Robert E.
Greaves, Joseph R.
Gregg, Hancock J.
Greiner, George.
Greland, John, Manager.
Greland, John F.
Greland, Titon, Director.
Grice, George W.
Grier, J. Mason.
Griffith, J. P.
Griffith, Robert E., M.D., Manager, Physician.
Griffiths, Samuel P., Manager.

Griffitts, Franklin P.
Grimes, John.
Groves, Daniel.
Gubert, Madame.
Gubert, Miss Louisa.
Gubert, T. E., Director.
Gulager, William.
Gummey, Thomas A.
Guthrie, Joseph M.
Gwinn, John.

Haedrich, Charles L.
Haedrich, Henry.
Hagedorn, Edward.
Hagedorn, Mrs. Edward.
Hagner, M. V.
Halbrach, Arnold.
Hall, James.
Hall, W. C.
Ham, Joseph W.
Hamer, Jacob.
Hampton, Alexander.
Hand, James C.
Hansell, William S.
Hansen, E. R.
Harding, Jesper.
Hare, J. C.
Hare, Robert, M.D.
Harmstead, James.
Harold, Alfred.
Harold, William.
Harper, Charles.
Harrington, Daniel.
Harris, Joseph B.
Harris, Lewitt.

MUSIC IN PHILADELPHIA

Harris, Thomas, M.D.
Harrison, Joseph.
Harrison, John H.
Harrison, William.
Harrold, F.
Hart, Abram L., Manager.
Hart, Hyman M.
Hart, Theodore M.
Hartley, John M.
Harvey, George N.
Haslam, Mrs. C. E.
Hassler, Henry.
Hassler, Isaac.
Hassler, Simon.
Hausman, Benjamin.
Hausman, C. F.
Haven, Charles C.
Haven, T. A.
Haviland, John.
Hawkins, Wm., Manager.
Hays, Henry.
Hays, Isaac, M.D., Manager, Physician.
Heberton, G. D.
Helé, James E.
Helmuth, George.
Hemphill, Robert J.
Henderson, James.
Henry, Julien.
Hepty, F.
Hertzog, Peter.
Hewitt, Miss Ann Eliza.
Heylin, Isaac, M.D.
Heysham, Robert.
Hickman, Nathaniel.

Hill, R. C.
Hill, W. K.
Hirst, James M.
Holmes, John.
Hollerman, John F.
Hollingsworth, Samuel.
Hollinsworth, T. G.
Hommann, J. C., Director, Manager.
Hommann, J. C., Jr.
Hood, William.
Hope, Isaac.
Hopewell, E.
Hopkins, Thomas.
Hopkinson, Francis.
Hopkinson, John S.
Hopkinson, Oliver.
Hopkinson, O. S.
Horner, Wm. E., M.D.
Houston, Joseph.
Houston, John M.
Houston, J. W., Secretary, 1822–27.
Houston, H. H.
Howell, Miss Beulah.
Hubbs, John E.
Hubbs, Paul K.
Hubner, F. A.
Hudson, Edward, Manager.
Hudson, Mrs. E.
Hüttner, Frederick, M.D., Director.
Hughes, Rev. John.
Hughes, Thomas.

MUSICAL FUND SOCIETY

Hugner, Charles V.
Humphreys, Sterne.
Hunneker, John.
Hupfeld, Chas. F., Director.
Hupfeld, John.
Hurley, Michael, D.D.
Hurst, Edward J.
Hutchinson, Randall.

Innis, F. B.
Ivanoff, Theodore.
Izard, Alicie.
Izard, Gen. George.
Izard, Ralph.

Jackson, Samuel, M.D.
James, J.
James, Thomas C., Manager.
Jandon, Samuel.
Jankie, John W.
Jarvis, Charles.
Jenke.
Jenks, Watson.
Jennings, John.
Jewell, John B., Jr.
Jewell, Leonard.
Johnson, Miss Jane.
Johnson, S. R.
Johnson, W. A.
Johnson, Walter R.
Johnston, Joseph S.
Jones, George B.
Jones, George F., Manager.
Jones, Horatio.

Jones, John T.
Jones, Joseph.
Jones, Thomas C.
Jones, William J.
Jordan, John, Jr.
Jordan, Thomas.

Kane, John K., Manager, Director, Counsellor; Secretary, 1820-21; Vice-President, 1829-34, 1838-50; President, 1854-56.
Kane, Mrs. John K.
Kane, Thomas L., Counsellor, Manager.
Karsten, John H., M.D.
Kay, James, Jr., Manager.
Kayser, John C.
Kayser, John G., M.D.
Keating, John, Jr., Manager, Counsellor.
Keating, William H., M.D., Vice-President, 1834-36.
Keating, William H., Jr., Counsellor.
Keen, Charles.
Kellner, August.
Kelly, Miss.
Kennedy, Isaac P.
Kester, George.
Keyser, Elhanan W., Director, Manager; Vice-President, 1853-54, 1856-60.
Kid, Robert C.

MUSIC IN PHILADELPHIA

King, John.
Kingston, Stephen.
Kittera, Thomas, Counsellor.
Klemm, F. A.
Klemm, John George, Director.
Kneass, William.
Knox, J. A.
Koecker, Leonard.
Koppetz, M. C.
Korkhaus, Andrew.
Korndofer, A.
Krollman.
Krumbhaar, Lewis, Jr.
Krumbhaar, William.
Krumbhaar, William, Jr.
Kugler, Lewis.
Kuhl, Henry.
Kuhn, Charles, Manager.
Kuhn, Chas., Jr., Manager.
Kuhn, Hartman.
Kuhn, Hartman, Jr.

Labbé, C. F.
Lafitte, John L., Director.
La Forgne, Miss Eliza.
Laguerrenne, P. L.
Lajus, Paul.
Lammot, Daniel, Treasurer, 1820.
Lancaster, J. B.
Lancaster, Thomas.
Lapsley, J. B.
La Roche, René, Jr., M.D., Physician, Director.
La Roche, Mrs. René.
Lasalle, Stephen B.
Latimer, James.
Laval, Mrs. John.
Lawrence, William P.
Lee, Isaac, Manager.
Leaming, Thomas F.
Le Brun, N., Manager.
Leedom, J. J.
Le Folle, J., Director.
Lehman, E. M.
Lehman, George S.
Lehman, Sylvanus.
Lehman, William.
Leiper, Miss A. G.
Lennard, Wm. J.
Lennig, Nicholas.
Leonard, James.
Le Roy, J. B.
Leslie, Charles M. F.
Levan, W.
Levering, Charles H.
Levering, Edward.
Levering, Joseph S.
Levy, E. S.
Lewis, David, Jr.
Lewis, George.
Lewis, George T.
Lewis, J. L.
Lewis, John T.
Lewis, Lewis.
Lewis, Mordecai D.
Lewis, Richard A.

MUSICAL FUND SOCIETY

Lewis, S. W.
Lewis, Wm. D., Manager.
Lewis, W. J.
Lex, Charles E., Director.
Lex, Jacob, Manager.
Lex, Jacob H.
Linn, John H.
Linnard, J. M.
Linnard, Thomas M.
Lippincott, William.
Littell, E.
Littell, John.
Littell, S., M.D.
Lohman, J.
Long, Major S. H.
Longstreth, C. S.
Lorich, Major L.
Loud, John.
Loud, Philologus.
Loud, Thomas, Director.
Lovering, Joseph S.
Lowber, Edward, M.D.
Lowber, John C.
Lowber, William T.
Lloyd, Samuel.
Luke, William.
Lukens, Isaiah.
Lukens, Israel.
Lybrand, P. S.
Lynch, William, Jr.
Lynd, James.

Mackey, C. C.
Mactier, Wm. L.
Madeira, Louis C., Manager; Secretary, 1856–58.
Maitland, Peter J.
Mallet, F. D.
Mange, Samuel.
Manning, Thomas.
Manuel, E.
Marchmant, H.
Markoe, James.
Markoe, Mrs. John.
Marks, Hyman.
Maris, Richard, M.D.
Maris, Thomas R.
Marsh, William.
Marshall, Gilbert.
Martel, Charles.
Martien, J. W.
Martien, William S.
Martin, George.
Martin, John B.
Marx, J. P.
Matthews, Mrs. Alecia.
Mayer, F. W.
Mayer, Rev. Philip.
Mayers, M.
McClellan, George, M.D.
McCready, J., M.D.
McCull, Henry, Counsellor.
McEwen, Charles.
McFarland, James B.
McGinley, D. B.
McGowden, John.
McGowen, J.
McIlhenney, J. E.

MUSIC IN PHILADELPHIA

McIlhenney, William J., Director, Manager; Secretary, 1821-22.
McIlvaine, Bloomfield.
McIlvaine, William.
McKean, Miss Mary.
McKinley, E.
McLane, Allan.
McLeod, Mrs. Isabella.
McMain, J. W.
McMurtrie, James.
McPherson, E. M.
Meade, Miss Henrietta.
Meade, Richard W.
Meade, Mrs. Richard W.
Meignen, Leopold, Director.
Meigs, Charles, M.D.
Melizet, J. M.
Meredith, William.
Merrick, John.
Merrick, Samuel V., Manager.
Messchert, H., Jr.
Messchert, M. H.
Mifflin, Benjamin.
Mifflin, Charles, M.D.
Miles, James.
Millard, James.
Miller, A. J.
Miller, Clement S.
Miller, D. S.
Miller, John J.
Miller, T. George.
Milnor, J. R.
Milnor, Robert.
Milnor, Thomas.
Mintzer, Charles A.
Mitchell, John K., M.D.
Mitcheson, D. W.
Montelius, William., Manager.
Montgomery, John C., Manager.
Moore, Marmaduke.
Moore, W.
Morgan, Thomas W.
Morris, Caspar W.
Morris, Robert.
Morrison, George.
Morrison, William M.
Morse, Henry.
Mortimer, John.
Morton, George, M.D.
Morton, Samuel G., M.D.
Moses, Isaac.
Moss, E. L.
Moss, John.
Muhlenberg, Rev. A.
Muhlenberg, Frederick A.
Muller, Augustus.
Muller, M.
Mumford, C. F.
Murray, James W.
Musser, Anna S.
Mütter, Thomas D., M.D., Physician.
Myerle, David.
Myers, William.

MUSICAL FUND SOCIETY

Nathans, Nathan.
Negus, James.
Neill, John, M.D., Physician.
Nevins, James.
Nevins, J. West, Manager.
Nevins, Richard.
Nevins, Samuel.
Newbold, John L.
Newman, Thomas.
Nicholas, Charles J., Director.
Nichols, A. St. Clair.
Nicklin, Philip H.
Nidelet, Stephen F.
Norris, Isaac.
Norris, Joseph P., Jr.
Norris, William., Jr., Director.
Norwell, John.
Notman, John.
Nowell, James.
Nulty, E.
Nunes, John F.

Oldmixon, William H.
O'Neill, John.
Otis, Bass.
Otto, Jacob.
Otto, Janet.

Page, James.
Palacio, J.
Palmer, Charles C.

Palmer, Thomas H., Director.
Pancoast, Miss M.
Parke, Miss Hannah.
Parke, James P.
Parsons, John G.
Patton, John C.
Patrallo, Nicholas.
Patrallo, Mrs. N.
Patterson, James V., M.D.
Patterson, Dr. Robert M., Vice-President, 1820-29, 1836-38; President, 1838-53.
Patterson, Mrs. Robert M.
Patterson, Robert, Manager.
Patterson, Robert L.
Patterson, W. O.
Paxon, J. R.
Pchellas, John F.
Peabody, George F.
Peace, Joseph, M.D., Physician.
Peacock, Gibson.
Peale, Franklin, Director.
Peale, Titian.
Pearson, Henry B.
Pechin, John C.
Peddle, W. A.
Peixoto, A. C.
Peneveyre, Charles.
Pennington, John.
Percival, Thomas C., Manager.

MUSIC IN PHILADELPHIA

Perdriaux, H.
Perdriaux, Peter, Director.
Perics, Adolphus.
Perkins, S. H.
Perrelli, Natalie.
Perrine, F.
Perring, L.
Perris, E. H.
Persico, Jean.
Peters, Richard, Jr.
Phillips, Mrs. Isaac.
Phillips, J.
Phillips, John S.
Phillips, Miss S.
Pierie, J. G.
Pierie, W. S.
Piers, G. R.
Pleasanton, Augustus.
Pleasants, Samuel.
Plitt, George.
Pohl, Paul.
Pollard, A., Jr.
Pollock, W. N.
Poole, A. R.
Potter, Sheldon.
Potts, Rev. George C.
Potts, Percival M.
Poulson, Charles A., Manager.
Poulson, Mrs. Charles A.
Poultney, Charles W.
Poval, Richard, M.D.
Powell, George.
Preiser, J. B.
Prevost, Henry M.

Price, John M.
Pringle, Miss Mary.
Prinzet, S. D.
Prud'homme, D. F.
Purry, Rowland.

Rainhard, John.
Ralston, Ashbel.
Ralston, Gerard, Manager.
Randall, Josiah.
Randolph, E.
Randolph, William.
Read, James, Jr., Manager.
Read, John M.
Read, William B.
Redwood, William.
Reed.
Reese, Jacob.
Reeve, Mark M., M.D., Physician.
Reeves, Thomas.
Rehn, Casper.
Rehn, G. T.
Reinhart, Adolph, Director.
Remington, Clement.
Rice, Rev. John.
Richards, Benjamin W.
Richards, Mark, Manager.
Richards, Thomas S.
Richardson, W. C.
Riehle, John.
Rielly, Captain Thomas.
Rinch, Francis.
Rinch, Louis.

MUSICAL FUND SOCIETY

Ritter, Abraham, Director, Manager.
Ritter, A., Jr.
Ritter, G. W.
Ritter, Jacob.
Robb, Samuel.
Robbins, S. J., Manager.
Roberts, Charles F.
Roberts, Edward.
Roberts, Thomas P., Manager.
Rockhill, A. C.
Roellig, M.
Rogers, Judge M. C.
Roppé, C. A.
Rosengarten, George D.
Rubicam, J.
Ruddach, D. J.
Rudiman, W. C., Jr.
Rudolph, C. F.
Rundle, Miss Frances.
Rundle, George, Manager.
Runkle, Theo.
Rush, James, M.D., Physician.
Rush, William, M.D.
Russell, J. S.
Ryan, L.

Samuel, David.
Sanderson, Joseph M.
Sandford, John W.
Sanford, John W.
Sarrazin, Mrs. Lucretia.
Savage, John.

Say, Benjamin, Manager.
Schaffer, W. L.
Scherer, L.
Scherr, E. N.
Schetky, Miss Caroline.
Schetky, George, Manager, Director.
Schively, Henry.
Schmidt, V. A.
Schmitz, Adolph, Director.
Seixas, A.
Sergeant, David.
Sellers, Charles.
Sellers, George E.
Shackeford, Mrs. Maria.
Shackelford, A. H.
Shaffer, G. S.
Sharpe, H. J.
Shaw, W. H.
Shaw, William, M.D.
Sheaff, H. W.
Sheepshanks, Miss Caroline.
Shewell, L. D.
Shivers, Thomas.
Short, William.
Shull, John B.
Sidebotham, John.
Simmons, Samuel.
Simpson, Henry.
Sinis, Robert.
Siter, John, Jr.
Skerrett, David C., M.D., Physician.

MUSIC IN PHILADELPHIA

Skerrett, James J., Manager.
Skinner, Rev. Thomas H.
Slaymaker, Stephen C.
Small, Robert H.
Smith, Aaron.
Smith, B. S., M.D.
Smith, Charles.
Smith, Charles S.
Smith, Francis Gurney, Manager, Treasurer, 1820-64.
Smith, Mrs. F. G.
Smith, Francis Gurney, M.D., Physician, 1820-64.
Smith, Gurney.
Smith, G. Washington, Manager.
Smith, Harrison.
Smith, James D.
Smith, Jesse.
Smith, Richard S., Manager.
Smith, Robert, Manager.
Smith, Mrs. R. S.
Smith, S. Decatur, Manager, Director.
Smith, William.
Smith, W. H.
Smith, William P.
Smith, William S., Manager, Director.
Smith, William Sydney.
Smith, William T.
Snelling, J. B.
Snider, Jacob.
Snowden, Dr. Isaac.
Snowden, J. Ross.
Solomon, Henry.
Souder, E. A.
South, George W.
Sparks, Thomas.
Spencer, Asa.
Sperry, Miss Maria.
Stacey, David B.
Stanbury, A. P.
Standbridge, A. T.
Standbridge, J. C. B., Director.
Stanley, Norris.
Starr, Isaac.
Steele, Albert W.
Steele, John.
Steele, John, Jr.
Stellwagon, Charles.
Stephenson, Rowland.
Stevenson, William W.
Stewart, Thomas.
Stewart, William H.
Stiles, Thomas.
Stillé, Benjamin.
Stockman, Jacob.
Stockton, S. A.
Stoll, William.
Stolte, C. F., Director.
Stone, Asaph.
Stone, C. H.
Stone, J.
Stratton, W. A.

MUSICAL FUND SOCIETY

Strickland, William, Manager.
Strickland, Mrs. William.
Stroup, William T.
Struthers, John.
Stutgard, Isaac.
Sulger, Miss Margaret.
Sullivan, John T. S., Director, Counsellor.
Sully, Thomas, Director.
Swaberg, J. W.
Swaim, James.
Swift, John.
Sykes, Robert W.
Sylvester, N.

Taitt, Samuel.
Taitt, W.
Tanner, Henry S.
Tatem, Miss Emily A.
Taws, Miss Henrietta.
Taws, John.
Taws, Joseph C., Director.
Taylor, George M., Director.
Taylor, Raynor, Director.
Taylor, Robert.
Tesseire, Anthony.
Thackara, William.
Thackara, William W.
Thein, Christopher.
Thomas, Joseph M.
Thomas, Moses.
Thomas, Samuel H.
Thompson, A. W.

Thompson, W. E.
Thorbecke, Herman.
Throckmorton, E.
Tiers, T. B.
Tilghman, Benjamin.
Tilghman, B.
Tingley, B. W.
Togno, Joseph, M.D.
Toland, Henry.
Toland, Robert.
Tolbert, John.
Torrey, S.
Towne, John H.
Townsend, John K.
Traquair, Adam.
Trautwine, J. A. C.
Treichel, Charles.
Trevor, Miss.
Trevor, John B.
Troutman, L. M.
Trucson, George E.
Tschirner, L. A.
Tucker, George.
Tunis, Robert R.

Uhlman, J.
Underwood, Thomas, Manager.

Vanderkemp, J. J.
Vansyckle, P. S.
Vaughn, John.
Verou, Thomas.
Vezin, Charles.
Vezin, Charles.

MUSIC IN PHILADELPHIA

Viereck, J. C.
Vinton, C. A.

Wagner, John.
Wagner, James D.
Wainwright, J.
Waldron, N.
Walker, Joseph.
Walker, E. L.
Walkins, Charles.
Wallace, J. W.
Walmsley, William D.
Walmsley, Wm. Mason, Manager.
Waln, Lewis.
Walters, A. G.
Warder, John R.
Ware, Lewis S.
Waterman, E.
Waterman, Isaac S.
Watmough, E. C.
Watson, Charles C.
Watson, Francis.
Watson, Henry R.
Weaver, George.
Webb, L. W.
Webb, W. H.
Webster, Thomas, Jr.
Weiland, F.
Weisse, John D.
Welch, Joseph.
Welford, Robert.
Welsh, John R.
Welsh, Samuel.
Wetherill, Christopher.

Wetherill, John P.
Whale, Henry.
Wharton, Francis R.
Wharton, John.
Wharton, Thomas J.
Wheeler, John.
Whelen, Townsend.
White, Britain.
White, David.
White, Henry R.
White, John.
Whitesides, William.
Wilcocks, Alex., M.D., Physician.
Wilcox, Edmund.
Wilhelm, Frederick.
Wilkinson, George.
Wilks, Benjamin G. S.
Williamson, Michael.
Willig, George.
Willing, Mrs. Augusta.
Willing, George C.
Wilmer, John R.
Wilmer, J. Ringold.
Wiltberger, Theo. N.
Winner, Septimus.
Wistar, Richard.
Wistar, Mrs. Richard.
Woglam, P.
Wolfe, Aaron.
Wolfe, J. K.
Wolle, Rev. Peter.
Wolsieffer, P. M.
Womrath, George F.
Wood, Joseph.

MUSICAL FUND SOCIETY

Wood, Richard C.
Woodward, J. S.
Woodward, W. H.
Woolworth, Robert.
Worley, F.
Worrell, Albert.
Worrell, J.
Worrell, J. C.
Worrell, Joseph.

Wright, Charles.
Wright, John B.
Wright, J. M.
Wright, Jonathan M., Director.
Wright, Thomas A.
Wylie, Rev. S. B.

Zantzinger, George.

INDEX

Academy of Fine Arts, 106.
Academy of Music, 152.
Acis and Galatea, Serenata, by Händel, 91.
Adams, John, 24, 25.
Alboni, 160.
Amodio, 170, 173.
Antognini, Cerillo, 151, 153.
Artôt, 150.
Astley, Thomas, 59, 63.
Athenian Institute, 119-121.
Austin, Mrs., 127, 139.

Bach, 98.
Badiale, Césare, 167.
Baptists, 24.
Bazaar, for the benefit of the Musical Fund Society, 157-160.
Beethoven, 57, 68, 73, 98, 104, 109, 130, 144, 152, 153, 154, 155, 168.
Billings, W., 36.
Binney, Horace, 118.
Bishop, Madame, 159.
Bishop, Sir Henry, 73, 80, 104.
Bishop White, 19-21, 118.
Boccherini, 57, 98, 104.
Boieldieu, 103.
Bradford's "Pennsylvania Journal," 29, 31.
Braham, John, 137, 140.
Brenan, M. E., 60, 63.
Brignoli, 160, 170, 172.
British Officers under General Howe in Philadelphia, 33.
Brown, David Paul, 119.
Bull, Ole, 148, 149, 151.
Burke, Mrs., 79, 80.
Bush Hill, 38.

Campbell, George, 165, 174.
Caradori Allen, Madame, 109, 138, 139.
Carpenters' Court, 63, 67, 69, 80, 82.
Carpenters' Hall, 63, 91.
Carpenters' Society, 75.
Carr, Benjamin, 22, 42, 49, 50, 52, 58, 59, 60, 62, 71, 72, 76, 83, 87, 107, 112, 124.
Carr, Thomas, 56.

INDEX

Casella, 150.
Castellan, Madame, 150.
Cherubini, 98, 146.
Chopin, 155, 161.
Christ Church, 18, 19.
Clementi, 98.
College of Philadelphia, 30, 31.
Composers, Early, 36.
Continental Congress, 32, 33.
Cross, Benjamin, 59, 60, 83, 106, 124, 173.
Cross, Benjamin C., 139.
"Creation," by Haydn, 56, 68, 78, 79, 81, 82, 84, 87, 91, 103, 104, 144, 146, 162.

"Daily Advertiser," Poulson's, 109.
Damoureau, Madame Cinti, 150.
Darley, J. C., 50, 54.
Darley, John, 38.
Dempster, 159.
Dettingen Te Deum, by Händel, 91, 95, 96, 97.
De Wees, Dr. Wm. P., 57, 58, 59, 67, 76.
Donizetti, 154.
Duponceau, Peter S., 57.

Eckert, Carl, 167.
Elliott's Hotel, 67.

Elsler, Fanny, 149.
Episcopal Church, 18-21

Feron, Madame, 127.
Fisher, Joseph, 58.
Franklin, Benjamin, 48, 49.
Franklin's "Pennsylvania Gazette," 29.
French, Mrs., 80, 83, 84, 86.
Friends' Yearly Meeting in 1716, 17.
Furness, Rev. Wm. H., 120, 121.

Gallatin, 114.
Gallupi, 98.
Garcia Opera Troupe, 108.
German Musical Societies, 166.
Germania Orchestra, 161, 167.
Gilles, P., 57, 58, 60, 63, 71, 80, 83.
Gillingham, George, 39, 43, 68.
Glossop, Mrs., 126.
Gluck, 105, 108, 146.
Gottschalk, 160, 161, 170.
Grisi, 160, 170, 171.

Händel, 41 (see "Messiah"), 52, 80, 87, 91, 95, 97, 98, 103, 105, 137.
Händel and Haydn Society, 68, 79, 127.

INDEX

Hallam Company of English actors, 27-30, 32, 34-35.
Hallam, Lewis, 27-30.
Handelian Society, 55.
Harmonica, or Musical Glasses, 48.
Harmonic Society, 54, 55.
Harpsichord, 46.
Harrowgate Garden, 38.
Haydn (see "Creation"), 37, 42, 57, 79, 81, 82, 83, 89, 98, 103, 104, 108, 144, 153.
Hensler, 160, 170, 171, 173.
Herz, Henri, 155, 161.
Hommann, John C., 58, 60, 76, 107; John, 58; Charles, 58, 76.
Horn, C. E., 126.
Howard, James, 131.
Hunt, Leigh, 48, 49.
Hupfeld, Charles P., 43, 49, 50, 51, 57, 58, 59, 60, 63, 71, 80, 83, 85, 106, 154.
Hupfeld, John, 57, 58.

Independent Harmonic Society, 55.
Instruments, Musical, 46-49, 84, 85.
Irving, Washington, 129.
Italian School, 103, 146, 147.

Jarvis, Charles, 124.
Jarvis, Charles H., 124.
Jaynes' Hall, 162.
Jefferson, Elizabeth, 103, 105.
Johnson's Band, 44, 45.
Julien, 166, 167.

Kane, John K., 57, 58, 59, 64-66, 143, 173.
Keyser, Elhanan W., 174.
Klemm, J. G., 83.
Koecker, Leonard, 57.

Lafayette, 43, 45, 46; Second Visit, 105.
Lagrange, 160, 170, 172, 173.
Lammot, Daniel, 59, 64.
Le Brun, 157.
Le Roy, 107.
Lind, 160, 164, 168, 169, 170.
Liszt, 155.
London Musical Fund Society, 61.
Longfellow, 171.
Loud, Thomas, 47, 48, 51, 58, 63, 71, 83, 107.
Lutheran: St. John's English Lutheran Church, 55.

Madeira, Louis C. (see Preface), 148, 166.

INDEX

Malibran, 107–109, 128, 170.
Maretzek's Opera House, 169.
Mario, 160, 170, 171.
Marshall, Chief-Justice, 114, 118.
Martini, 37.
Mehul, 76, 103, 146.
Meignen, L., 154.
Mendelssohn, 99, 155.
Mercantile Library Association, Course of Lectures, 120, 121.
"Messiah," by Händel, 36, 40, 42, 56, 109.
Methodists, 25.
Meyer, Leopold De, 154.
Meyerbeer, 154.
Moravians, 24, 25, 78, 79, 84.
Morelli, 172, 173.
Mozart, 57, 80, 89, 95, 98, 108, 139, 140, 144, 146, 153.
Music Stores, 43, 49, 80, 81.
Musical Fund Hall: Erection, 93-101; Lectures by Famous Men, 120-122; Orations and Political Meetings, 113-119; Enlargement, 157-160.
Musical Fund Society: Officers elected at First Meeting, 59; List of Original Members, 60, 66; Purpose, 62; Programme of First Concert, 70; Orchestra, 102, 104, 144, 146, 148, 152, 153, 154, 155; the "Academy," 104-107, 110-112, 143, 145.

National Amphitheatre, 168.
"National Gazette," 141.
Norma, 130.

Oldmixon, Mrs., 41; Sir John, 41.

Paer, 80, 104.
Paganini, 149, 150, 151.
Paine, Thomas, 49.
Palestrina, 98.
Patterson, Dr. Robert W., 57, 58, 59, 87.
Philadelphia, Musical Outlook, 174, 175.
Piano-forte, Manufacture, 46–48.
Pico, Rosina, 151, 153.
Plays, Early Performances, 26-30, 32-40.
Plumstead's Warehouse, 26.
Poole, Elizabeth, 139, 140.
Poulson, Charles C., 57-59.
"Poulson's Daily Advertiser," 85.

INDEX

Power, Tyrone, 127, 128.
Presbyterian Church, 22, 23; Second Presbyterian Church, 54; Fifth Presbyterian Church, 55, 93.
"President," the Ship Lost at Sea, 129.
Purcell, 97, 98.

Quakers, 18, 122.

Rawle, 119.
Reformed German Church, 36.
Reinagle, Alexander, 52.
Reis, 98.
Roman Catholic Church, 21, 22, 25.
Romberg, 71, 98.
Rovere, 172.
Rossi, 160.
Rossini, 72, 90, 108, 150, 172.
Russell, Henry, 131-138, 150.

Sanguirico, 150, 153.
St. Andrew's Church, 91.
St. Augustine's Church, 56.
St. Cecilia Society, 56.
St. Joseph's Roman Catholic Church, 21, 22.
St. Peter's Church, 50, 51, 52, 94.
St. Stephen's Church, 91.

Schetky, George, 49, 58, 59, 60, 63, 69, 71, 76, 87, 123, 124.
Schmitz, 107.
Schumann, 99, 151.
"Seasons," 146.
Seguin, Edward and Anne, 139, 140.
Sergeant, John, 115.
Shireff, Jane, 139.
Sivori, 151.
Smith, Francis G., 68.
Societies: Various Early Singing Societies, 54-56.
Sonnambula, 129, 131, 167, 168.
Sontag, 160, 165; her Reception, 165-168, 170.
Strickland, William, 50, 59, 94, 99.
Sully, Thomas, 53, 60, 95.
Symphony, First Performance in Philadelphia, 144, 145.

Taylor, Raynor, 43, 49, 51, 52, 60.
Theatre, Chestnut Street, 39, 41, 43, 45; New, in Water Street, 29; New, on Society Hill, 30; "Northern Liberties," 38; "Old South," or "Southwark," 30, 32, 34, 37.

INDEX

Union Harmonic Society, 55.
"United States Gazette," 109, 119.
University of Pennsylvania, 41, 52, 54, 91, 116, 117.
Uranian Society, 54.

Vauxhall Garden, 43.
Viardot, 170.
Vieuxtemps, 150, 151, 154.

Wallace, W. V., 150.
Washington, George, 22, 36, 37, 38.
Washington Hall, 69, 70, 79, 81, 83, 84, 88, 92, 100.
Weber, 109, 131, 155, 167.
Webster, Daniel, 169.
Weisse, J. D., 76, 84, 85.
Willis, Nathaniel P., 171.
Wood, Mr. and Mrs., 129-131, 139.

www.ingramcontent.com/pod-product-compliance
Lightning Source LLC
Chambersburg PA
CBHW030138170426
43199CB00008B/115